An Unexpected Journal

Image Bearers

Spring 2021

Volume 4, Issue 1

CONTENTS

Goodness, Truth and Beauty

L.B. Loftin on Humanity

Oh, what a Blessed race are we
Whose souls are nourished by Adjectival Waters
Freely flowing as brooks from a Substantive Sea.
Only by that water do we live, move and be.

INTRODUCING 'WORTH READING'

Jason Smith on a New Column Coming to AUJ

When C.S. Lewis was asked in 1944 to write the preface for a new edition of St. Athanasius' foundational 4th-century book *On the Incarnation*, Lewis felt it was important to begin by advocating for "reading old books," a practice that had fallen out of vogue amidst the heyday of Modernism. The result was a critical essay on how to train your mind to avoid being swept up in the fervors and frenzies of the moment in which you happen to live, to recognize the common errors of your particular *zeitgeist*, and to avoid falling into the trap of what Lewis and Owen Barfield called "chronological snobbery," which they defined as the unconscious assumption that modes of thought which have fallen out of fashion are necessarily inferior to the modes of thought which succeeded them. Lewis' essay is available in the collection *God in the Dock* as well as a recent re-issue of *On the Incarnation*.

Today, it becomes increasingly necessary to advocate for reading *books*, full stop. No need to belabor the point: there's already been plenty of hand wringing over drastic declines in reading since the 1950s as time spent watching TV shows has climbed.[1] (Undue attention has also been paid to the *very* modest amount that Millennials read more than older generations, thanks partly to ebooks and audio books).[2] Although more *words* are probably being read at any given moment now than at any previous point in history, most of the words that our eyes encounter are part of short-form pieces distributed digitally: emails, instant messages, blogs, texts, news articles, comics, think pieces, message boards, social media posts, memes, ads. Let's set aside the studies indicating that digital reading seems to take more effort both to understand and to remember than paper reading.[3] That research may not hold up

[1] Christopher Ingraham, "Leisure reading in the U.S. is at an all-time low." *The Washington Post*, June 29, 2018, accessed February 21, 2021, https://www.washingtonpost.com/news/wonk/wp/2018/06/29/leisure-reading-in-the-u-s-is-at-an-all-time-low/.

[2] Alison Flood, "Young read more books than older generation, research finds," *The Guardian*, September 12, 2014, accessed February 21, 2021, https://www.theguardian.com/books/2014/sep/12/young-read-more-books-than-older-generation-research.

[3] Ferris Jabr, "The Reading Brain in the Digital Age: The Science of Paper versus Screens," *Scientific American*, April 11, 2013, accessed

over time because of *neuroplasticity*, the term for how our brains rewire themselves to take better advantage of the tools we use regularly . . . which is cause for both amazement and concern. Too much time spent reading pithy content online may in fact be making it harder for us to read books.[4]

Which brings us to the central question: What is a book? Better yet, what is a *good* book? (Because for a book to be worth the time and attention it takes to read, it had better be good!)

When a book is "good," what job is it doing that other kinds of writing, other ways of organizing and presenting words, cannot?

A good book is a long-form organization of ideas, research, and narrative that explores complexity, develops thorough arguments and expansive themes, and treats delicate or sensitive material in a nuanced and illuminating manner, when any of the above would be impossible in a shorter work.

February 21, 2021, https://www.scientificamerican.com/article/reading-paper-screens/.

[4] Michael S. Rosenwald, "Serious reading takes a hit from online scanning and skimming, researchers say," *The Washington Post*, April 6, 2014, accessed February 21, 2021, https://www.washingtonpost.com/local/serious-reading-takes-a-hit-from-online-scanning-and-skimming-researchers-say/2014/04/06/088028d2-b5d2-11e3-b899-20667de76985_story.html.

To turn that around and look at it from another angle, a good book is book-length because it must be. It demands that the reader be mentally immersed in its pages over an extended period of time because doing justice to the raw material of its story or its argument requires immersion. A good book must engage the mind on a single subject and pull it upstream on a river of insight or experience over hours and days so that the living brain can reshape itself and become able to understand and appreciate the author's craft and message.

(By the way, a great book on appreciating craft and message is Lewis's *Experiment in Criticism*. Despite the academic-sounding title, it's an accessible read).

Short-form writing cannot do a good book's job. It's too ephemeral. We skim it, extract a few key phrases, perhaps copy the link to some friends, and move on.[5] If we want to better understand the awesome complexities of our world, develop empathy for someone with a complicated life experience (and whose life experience isn't complicated?), or even gain insight into our own

---

[5] Farhad Manjoo, "You Won't Finish This Article," *Slate*, June 6, 2013, accessed February 21, 2021, https://slate.com/technology/2013/06/how-people-read-online-why-you-wont-finish-this-article.html.

psyches, good books are a great option -- often, the only option.[6] Relying on the ephemera of short-form content, even though it can be entertaining and informative, saps our mental and emotional ability to engage with a nuanced subject over a long time. Neil Postman warned -- with insight that has long seemed prophetic -- of the societal consequences of neglecting the discipline of long-form attentiveness in his 1985 book *Amusing Ourselves to Death*. Almost 40 years later, we find ourselves in dire need of men and women capable of parsing complexity, appreciating nuance, and engaging others with empathy.

OK; let's say we're convinced. But here's the real problem: where to start? Somewhere between 2 and 3 million new books are published every year, including reprints and new editions. Our time and attention are finite. Which books deserve it? What's worth reading?

We're all asking this question. One of the best ways to answer it is through crowdsourcing: using the recommendations of other like-spirited readers

---

[6] Claudia Hammond, "Does reading fiction make us better people?" *BBC*, June 2, 2019, accessed February 21, 2021, https://www.bbc.com/future/article/20190523-does-reading-fiction-make-us-better-people.

with similar interests to narrow the list of potentials to a manageable size.

Therefore: this column. Our hope is to turn this space, issue by issue, into a proverbial threshing floor that separates the wheat from the chaff.

Going forward, we intend "Worth Reading" to become a regular fixture of *An Unexpected Journal*. It will feature book recommendations related to the theme of the issue in which each installment appears. Most of the titles featured won't be "hot off the presses." Some will be popular, bestselling titles. Others may be more obscure. We'll recommend books for kids, books for adults, fiction and nonfiction, all genres considered. What these books will have in common is what makes them Worth Reading: each does a job that only a book could do, and does it well.

We hope you'll look forward to this column in future issues, and we hope it will help guide you (and perhaps your friends and loved ones) to some really good books. But more than that, we hope you'll participate! Take a look at the upcoming issues listed on our submissions page. Then, use the submissions form to recommend a book. Include the title, author, and a short writeup (aim for 500 words or fewer) explaining how your recommendation fits the issue theme and why it fits this column's definition of a book Worth Reading.

MATRIX OF MEANING: FIVE THESES ON CHRISTIANITY AND CULTURE

Donald Williams on the Relationship between Human Nature and Creativity

The question of the proper relationship of the church to human culture cannot be avoided.

1. **Human beings are creative because they are made in the image of the Creator.** (We were made in God's image so that we could not only have fellowship with Him but so we would be qualified to represent Him as His sub-regents and stewards on earth.)

2. **Culture is the material, social, and symbolic matrix that results from the full range of mankind's creative activity.** (It includes business, carpentry, farming, and cooking as well as art, music, drama, and literature; all are seamless products of human creativity.)

3. **Culture is not and cannot be spiritually neutral or irrelevant.** (It flows from the very

heart of human identity as a creature made in the image of God to serve Him as stewards of His earth — or from our rebellion against that identity.)

4. **Francis Schaeffer was right to insist that part of Christian discipleship is living out "the Lordship of Christ over the total culture."** (Salvation is not just a religious "experience"; it restores us to our role as sub-creators for God's glory.)

5. **The Christian subculture in any society should bring salt and light to that society through its own cultural activity, both in creating and consuming culture.** (From homemaking to gardening to labor to art and music, the quality of our lives should reflect who we are.)

Introduction:

The Christian church was born out of an ancient Semitic culture into a pagan culture and has survived into a secularist and neo-pagan one in the West while expanding into every kind of cultural milieu imaginable across the planet. In the meantime it has been a major player in creating and molding culture, especially Western culture, and has had its influence on whatever culture it has entered. But the situation is complicated in that the influence unavoidably goes both ways. It is not always easy to discern what in contemporary Christendom represents universal and non-negotiable truths revealed by God and what reflects the culture into which those truths have to be incarnated. Another important question: When is that inevitable cultural flavoring a necessary and even positive reflection of the fact that the church has successfully indigenized itself incarnationally, and when is it a corruption of its basic principles?

We have not always done a good job of discerning the answers to such questions. Most people can see that nineteenth-century missionaries should not have automatically tried to get tribesmen to wear Western clothes or switch to Western styles of music. It is not hard to see that American Evangelicalism has been perhaps a bit too much influenced by American pragmatism and consumerism. But where do you draw the line? Not all cultural influence is mere imperialism by the Western church or a corruption of it by pagan or secularist values. Surely the Auca Indians are better off not to have a culture based on vendetta any longer; that is a direct impact of their conversion to

Christianity on their culture.[1] And surely current Christians should not wish to jettison Handel's *Messiah* because it uses musical techniques that were developed for the secular opera. (There were some Christians who protested it when it was first performed because they thought it impious to have the Gospel sung in a secular concert hall instead of a church.[2] They probably would have had a problem with Jesus preaching out on a hillside instead of in the synagogue, if the Sermon on the Mount were not already part of Scripture.)

Figuring out how the church should relate to culture and how it should seek to influence culture without being corrupted by it — figuring out how practically, in other words, for it to be in the world but not of it — is not an easy task. It includes, but is not limited to, how the church should relate to media and the arts. I think American Evangelicals need to do a better job of it and that no Reformation of that movement can be whole and wholesome otherwise. It will be easier if we can come to a theological understanding of what culture is and lay

---

[1] For more on this story, see Elisabeth Elliot, *Through Gates of Splendor* (Carol Stream, IL: Tyndale Momentum, 1981).

[2] Thomas E. Kaiser, "Handel's Messiah: Sacred or Profane?" *Praeclara*, accessed February 22, 2021, https://www.praeclara.org/?page_id=641.

down some basic principles that govern our unavoidable participation in it. That will be the task of these five theses.[3]

THESIS 1: HUMAN BEINGS ARE CREATIVE BECAUSE THEY ARE MADE IN THE IMAGE OF THE CREATOR.

Why does human culture exist? Why is it different in different places? Why does it have variations even in the same place? My ninth-grade history teacher defined culture as "the learned behavior of man, as he has adapted himself to his total environment." By that definition, every species has a "culture." But all robins make the same style

---

[3] The foundations for the understanding of culture proposed here are in J.R.R. Tolkien, "On Fairy Stories," *The Tolkien Reader* (N.Y. Ballantine, 1966), 3-84), and Dorothy L. Sayers, *The Mind of the Maker* (N.Y.: Harper and Row, 1968). The place to start for understanding a biblical relationship between Christianity and Culture is Francis Schaeffer's "cultural apologetic," laid out in *The God Who is There* (Downers Grove, IL: InterVarsity, 1968). Other important works wrestling with issues of Christianity and culture include Abraham Kuyper, *Lectures on Calvinism* (Grand Rapids: Eerdmans, 1931), H. Richard Niebuhr, *Christ and Culture* (N.Y.: Harper and Row, 1951), Henry R. Van Til, *The Calvinistic Concept of Culture* (Philadelphia: Presbyterian and Reformed, 1959), Francis Schaeffer, *Art and the Bible* (Downers Grove, IL.: InterVarsity, 1973), Leland Ryken, *Culture in Christian Perspective* (Portland: Multnomah, 1986), Andy Crouch, *Culture Making: Recovering our Creative Calling* (Downers Grove, IL.: InterVarsity, 2008), and Donald T. Williams, *Deeper Magic: The Theology Behind the Writings of C. S. Lewis* (Baltimore: Square Halo Books, 2016), pp. 201-14. A very helpful practical approach to realizing Christian culture on a personal level is Edith Schaeffer, *Hidden Art* (Wheaton, Tyndale, 1971).

and design of nest, while human beings live in caves, tents, houses, and other structures — and even the houses have an almost infinite variety of designs: log cabin, cottage, shot-house, ranch, Cape Cod, Victorian, neo-classical, Tudor half-timbered, with multiple variations on each of those styles. And while the secular mind emphasizes the continuity — we both build shelters — if a robin started really acting like a human being — making a hundred different styles of nest and, more significantly, making stick and clay statues of famous robins and decorating its nest with them — we should find him, as Chesterton says, a fearful wildfowl indeed.[4] What is the difference?

Human beings are creative in a way that transcends anything we see in the animal world. We do not, like animals, do things out of instinct and hence do them all the same way. And we do things they don't do at all. Cavemen drew pictures of reindeer on the walls of their caves. We have not found any deer drawing pictures of men. It is more than just a matter of intelligence. A monkey might break off a stick to use as a tool for digging termites

---

[4] G.K. Chesterton, *The Everlasting Man* (N.Y.: Dodd, Meade, 1925), 22. See this book for a fascinating analysis of why human beings differ from animals in this way; cf. Donald T. Williams, *Mere Humanity* (Chilicothe, OH: DeWard, 2018), for more on Chesterton's apologetic.

out of a hill; he might arrange boxes into a pile he can climb to retrieve a banana hung from the ceiling. He surely shows a certain rudimentary intelligence in doing so. But he will not arrange the sticks or the boxes into a symmetrical pattern just so he can sit back and contemplate it, while getting no termites or bananas out of them at all. Birds sing (all the same tune) to look for a mate or mark their territory. "This is my tree! Go find your own!" They do not gather in flocks to listen to a particularly good warbler just because he sounds so cool. So, as Chesterton rightly and aptly concludes, "Art is the signature of man."[5]

It is understandable then that people often confuse culture with the arts. The arts are, in fact, a salient manifestation of human nature and hence of human culture. We are the only species that has art that exists only for contemplation and enjoyment and has no obvious pragmatic purpose. But it is the same creativity that makes us artists that also makes us unique as a species in science, in agriculture, in industry, in architecture, in homemaking, in politics — all areas in which individual and corporate human creativity generates the kind of world in which we live and affects the way we live in it. Creativity and the

---

[5] Chesterton, *Everlasting Man*, op. cit., 16.

culture it generates are central to who we are. In a sense, that is what makes us Man.

This radical discontinuity between us and the rest of the animal kingdom demands an explanation, and evolution is not capable of providing it. I am not going to enter into the controversy over precisely how much biological evolution contributed to the origin of our species except to observe that, while it clearly played some role, it cannot be the whole story. With all the physical continuity we have with other animals, we are not in the sum total of our nature just an incremental step further down the same road as them, but rather represent a right turn and a quantum leap. There is only one adequate explanation for that leap that I have ever seen, and Christians are privileged to have it in their possession — a tremendous advantage if they want to understand and properly relate to human culture. It is in the biblical doctrine of creation, particularly as elaborated by J.R.R. Tolkien in his concept of "sub-creation": we are creative because we were made in the image of the Creator.[6] God's "primary creation"

---

[6] Tolkien, "On Fairy Stories," op. cit. For further analysis of Tolkien's idea and how it relates to the biblical worldview, see Donald T. Williams, *Mere Humanity*, op. cit., esp. chp. 3, and also his *An Encouraging Thought: The Christian Worldview in the Writings of*

(the universe and us, in His image) leads to our "secondary creation" — of literature and art and music, but first of language itself, and then also of homes and furniture and meals and tools and cities. We, through our God-given creative impulses and energy, were designed to assist Him in bringing His creation to its full potential, to completeness and fruition — not because He needed assistance, but because, in His own creativity and personality, He desired graciously to share with us the joy of making the world. We were to fill the world (with our progeny and also the products of our labor), to subdue it, and to rule it on His behalf (Gen. 1:28). Theologians call this "the cultural mandate."

The creation of culture then is fulfilling to us because it is the expression of our God-given identity: it is who we are. Unfortunately, we rebelled against God in the Garden. As a result, we still rule the world, but for ourselves rather than for Him, and hence often rather badly. But masters of the earth we are still, or try to be, though by its thorns and thistles it does not cooperate with our rule as well as it once might have. Human culture then reflects human identity. We are created in the image of God

---

J.R.R. Tolkien (Cambridge, OH: Christian Publishing House, 2018), esp. chp. 2.

but fallen, hence both magnificent and wretched, totally depraved in terms of our ability to merit salvation through our own works and yet still retaining the ruins of our original goodness.[7] We still do much that is good (in a temporal, not in a spiritual or salvific sense) because the remnants of our original goodness still inhere in us and because of common grace.[8] But we also do much that is foolish or downright evil. As a result, human cultures, like human beings, are complex mixtures of good and evil. Culture cannot be simply rejected — we could not live without it — but neither can it be uncritically embraced. This applies to all cultures, though some may be more corrupt or more conducive to certain types of goods than others. This is what makes being "in the world but not of it" such a challenging proposition.[9] But it is not a challenge that we have the option to shirk.

---

[7] See Douglas Groothuis, *Christian Apologetics* (Downers Grove, IL: InterVarsity Press, 2011), chp. 18, for a fuller discussion of this point.

[8] *Common Grace* is a theological term for the way God graciously restrains the full results of sin in human beings and in human societies so that we are not as evil as our Fall would otherwise have made us — He "sends His rain upon the just and the unjust" (Mt. 5:45). It is called *common* grace because all benefit from it, as distinguished from special grace, or saving grace, which applies only to believers in Christ.

[9] John 17:14-16.

Two important conclusions follow from this understanding of the origins of culture. First, culture is significant. It is the central expression of our very identity, flowing from our unique status as created in the image of the Creator. That makes it important and powerful. But its power needs to be seen in the context of the second conclusion: cultural determinism is eliminated as a valid understanding of how we relate to culture. We cannot say that a person's culture *determines* how he will see the world and what he will do (despite many Post-Modernist analyses that imply that it does, if not stating so outright). Culture, and our "situatedness" in it, is indeed a powerful influence because it flows from the dynamic influence of human creativity. But precisely for that very same reason, we can never hide behind the mantra that, "My culture made me do it." We are the creators of culture and therefore are capable of standing above it. Many may not choose to do so; they may acquiesce in its influence as if it had created them. But if we create culture or, more accurately, participate in its creation, then it is ultimately subject to our judgment and susceptible to our free actions. Our feelings, beliefs, and acts are influenced by our culture but do not have to be bound by it. Our freedom as moral agents within culture then also flows from the image of God. Creativity means the ability to do things that are not purely the result of antecedent circumstances and influences — the ability to contribute something actually new. We were created in the image of the Creator.

THESIS 2: CULTURE IS THE MATERIAL, SOCIAL, AND SYMBOLIC MATRIX THAT RESULTS FROM THE FULL RANGE OF MANKIND'S CREATIVE ACTIVITY.

Now we are in a position to give a working definition of culture. The word comes from a Latin root whose most basic meaning is planting, tilling, growing crops. A *cultor* is a planter; *cultura* is tilling; *cultus* means tilling, cultivation. It is for this reason that the very word *culture* is a part of the word *agriculture.* The picture is that of human effort, directed by human intelligence, being expended onto nature to produce a result that nature by herself would not have given us: stalks of wheat or grapevines or olive trees concentrated in ordered rows in a field and growing in a literally unnatural abundance (an abundance that nature unaided could not have produced), there for our convenience to the end that human beings and human society might flourish. The picture is very consistent with the biblical account of human beings. We are creators, but sub-creators. Unlike God, we cannot bring something out of nothing. We have to depend on Him for some given (the natural world) to work with. But we bring forth from those natural raw materials results that nature by herself could not achieve: not primary creation, but real sub-creation. How long we lived as hunter-gatherers I do not know. But when agriculture emerged in human history, it emerged from the divinely imaged nature and creative potential that God had given us. So while the hunter-gatherers surely had culture (they made art and buried their dead with ceremony, for example), with agriculture a new level of culture became possible: what we call *civilization*.

Already in Latin the words *cultor*, *cultura*, and *cultus*, whose literal meanings we gave above, began very early to be used metaphorically to refer to the cultivation or development from their natural state into forms more beneficial (or harmful) to human beings of things other than crops: buildings, cities, arts, governments, religions, Man himself. Once this happens we are on the verge of the definition we would like to use here: *Culture is the material, social, and symbolic matrix that results from the full range of mankind's creative activity*. That is what we speak of today when we refer to a nation or a people or even a smaller group like a school, a church, or a business ("corporate culture") as having a culture. They have developed a way of doing things, making things, and relating to each other through that doing and making that characterizes their society. It is inherited but also constantly changing as their creative activity continues to have input, preserving, altering, improving, corrupting, sometimes even destroying that total way of being in the world. These culture-creating acts are largely unconscious, but sometimes are very conscious and deliberate. The resulting cultural matrix grows from the kind of creative activity that is characteristic of human beings because they were created in the image of the Creator. It includes but is not limited to what is sometimes called "high culture": painting, sculpture, fiction, poetry, theater, cinema, music, dance. It includes religion, business, carpentry, farming, cooking, media, and education along with what we call the "fine" arts; it also includes science. All are seamless products of human creativity. You could say it is the mark we leave on each other as we leave our mark on the world.

Now here's the point. We were created to do this. We have to do this. We don't have the option not to participate. It is not a sin to do this. It would be a sin not to do this, if not doing it were possible. Sin or virtue, obedience or disobedience, lies in *the way* we do it. Do we do it for God or for self? In accordance with and reflecting His revealed truth or in rebellion against and suppressing or distorting it? Submissive to His wisdom or insisting on our own folly? Sorting all that out is why we need three more theses.

THESIS 3. CULTURE IS NOT AND CANNOT BE SPIRITUALLY NEUTRAL OR IRRELEVANT.

Perhaps no one would *say* that culture is spiritually irrelevant. But many Evangelical Christians act as if they thought it were. They would think the idea of the church returning to its historic role as a patron, hence influencer, of the arts just silly. Meanwhile, they are entertained by music and sitcoms that undermine their biblical worldview and coarsen their manners, blissfully unaware that there is a problem with this. It does not help that the only alternative model they are aware of is the old Fundamentalist rejection of all "secular" culture as inherently evil and corrupting — for example, not using discernment but simply avoiding all public theater and popular music as part of "the world." That was a failure of spiritual responsibility in cultural engagement, an approach just as inadequate as their own. They rejected it (or their parents did — they may not even remember it) without putting any better model in its place. Their unthinking approach contributes greatly to their inability to be faithful to the content or practice of the faith they think they espouse.

Nevertheless, culture is not and cannot be spiritually neutral or irrelevant. It flows from the very heart of human identity as a creature made in the image of God to serve Him as stewards of His earth — or from our rebellion against that identity. Our relationship to culture is thus inevitably complicated. God supports culture because it nurtures His human creatures, who could not live without it. Even the worst and most corrupt cultures contain much that is good by common grace — which no doubt pleases Him. Nevertheless, God also stands in judgment over culture because it is the reflection not only of mankind's identity as created in His image but also of its identity as a rebel against His service.

A seemingly confusing biblical metaphor reflects this dual nature of culture and thus creates a tension for God's people in this complex world. Christians, His redeemed children, are to see themselves as strangers and exiles in such fallen cultures (Heb. 11:13, 1 Pet. 2:11), but they are also to follow in the steps of their Israelite forebears and "seek the welfare of the city where [they] have been sent into exile and pray to the Lord on its behalf," be it Babylon, Nineveh, or Rome (Jer. 29:7). They are neither to identify with human culture nor to stand aloof from it. In other words, this dual role implies that they are to be participating in this foreign culture, not withdrawing from it; but at the same time they should not be finding their primary identity in it, yielding themselves to its influence uncritically, or allowing themselves to be defined by it. They are to be in it but not of it (John 17:14-15). To navigate this dual role successfully, they cannot have an intellectually lazy approach. The path of least resistance is not open to them. They must constantly be exercising *discernment*. That is why Reformation is needed in this area. We *are* intellectually lazy. It is easy to yield to culture; it is relatively easy to convince yourself that you have withdrawn from it. (You will not have, of course, not really.) On neither of those paths is there any spiritual integrity, salt and light, or credible witness to be found. Where are these things found?

Somehow we must be "in" the world and "not of" it at the same time; somehow we must achieve the integration of these two prepositions in one unified lifestyle that becomes the mark of *Christian* culture. But that is difficult. What we often attempt is the much easier task of taking one of these prepositions in isolation from the other. It requires no effort at all to be "in" the world; the path of least resistance will suffice to accomplish that most efficiently. And, while it requires more effort, it is also possible to be "not of" the world, up to a point. Here we create our (partially) insulated parallel universe, with borders guarded by ever-increasing lists of Rules. "We don't cuss, drink, smoke, or chew, / And we don't go with girls that do." We create our own little Christian ghetto and withdraw within its borders so we will not be corrupted. We write our own music and books and create our own TV, all of which somehow turn out to be strangely cheap imitations of what the world is doing but without the grosser forms of immorality. But this is a false approach, and Christ makes it clear he does not mean us to take it. He does so both by his prayer in John 17:15 ("I do not ask You to take them out of the world, but to keep them from the evil one") and by his example, hanging out with publicans and sinners and scandalizing the religious conservatives of his day.

We can pursue either of these prepositions in the flesh. We do not have in ourselves either the wisdom or the strength to be "in" and "not of" at the same time. That requires the wisdom and the power of God; that requires discernment and dying to self. And so, of course, it is not to be thought of by half-hearted Christians, and so it is seldom seen.

Yet that is precisely what is commanded: not isolated prepositions in the flesh, but the integration of the two prepositions in the Spirit. But how can we do that? Paul provides the answer; "Finally, brethren, whatever is true, whatever is honorable, whatever is right, whatever is pure, whatever is lovely, whatever is of good repute, if there is any excellence, and if anything worthy of praise, let your mind dwell on these things" (Phil. 4:8)

What kind of command is this verse? It is a Positive Command. It is about what we are positively supposed to have our minds dwell on. But in our application of it we have almost universally turned it into a negative command, about what we are not supposed to read, watch, or listen to: "Oh, this is impure, so I'd better stay away from it!" Why have we managed to be so inattentive to what the Text actually says? Because it is easier. It is easier to boycott all movies (or all movies of a certain rating) than to use discernment; it is easier to swear off of "secular" music or "rock" than to listen critically to what the world is actually saying through these media, understand with empathy the cries of its lost voices, but then choose the good and dwell on that.

I repeat: this verse says not one word about what we cannot read, watch, or listen to. It says not a single word about what we must turn a blind eye to, pretend isn't there, or be ignorant of. It says a lot about what we should nourish and feed our minds on. Contrary to the T-shirt, Nietzsche isn't preachy; he is actually very preachy, and what he is preaching is straight from the Pit. But he has been very influential and he is important, and even in his evil he can teach us some things. Therefore, I was not disobeying this passage when I read him, even though he is rightly described by none of the adjectives (except possibly "excellent," in the sense of "outstanding") that the verse recommends. But that is not the kind of thing I feed my mind on constantly. What is? I read Tolkien's *The Lord of the Rings* twice in 1968, the year I discovered it, and have read it annually since as a way of cleaning out the garbage that has collected in my mind from grading freshman essays and reconnecting myself with the Good, the True, and with the Beautiful, with the contrast between Good and Evil, with the nature of the Quest, and the value and significance of Sacrifice.[10] No work speaks more eloquently and powerfully to me of such things. More importantly,

---

[10] See my book An Encouraging Thought: The Christian Worldview in the Writings of J.R.R. Tolkien (Cambridge, OH: Christian Publishing House, 2018) for more on these themes in The Lord of the Rings.

I am doing the same thing with Scripture on a daily basis. That is what the verse is talking about.

It is not that there is nothing that is so raw, so evil, so corrupting that we should not expose ourselves to it. There is much that falls in that category, and the increasing decadence of our society can render us appallingly naïve at discerning what it is. But our main strategy for dealing with these problems is too often negative while the Bible's is positive. Understanding this distinction makes Phil. 4:8 the answer to the dilemma raised by Jesus' words in John 17. How do we live "in" the world without becoming "of" it? We do it through a positive, pro-active program of feeding ourselves on the good. Do not focus primarily on what you cannot read, watch, or listen to. Do not use ignorance as the path to safety. Machen put it well: "Some of modern thought must be refuted. The rest must be made subservient. But nothing in it can be ignored."[11] Rather, the formula is this: Really feed your mind on the Good, True, and Beautiful, as defined by Scripture and exemplified in the best of the classical tradition, and then it will respond rightly to the rest.

---

[11]J. Gresham Machen, *Education, Christianity, and the State* (Unicoi, Tn.: The Trinity Foundation, 1987), 57.

THESIS 4: FRANCIS SCHAEFFER WAS RIGHT TO INSIST THAT PART OF CHRISTIAN DISCIPLESHIP IS LIVING OUT "THE LORDSHIP OF CHRIST OVER THE TOTAL CULTURE."

If human culture exists as the product of human creativity because human beings were created in the image of the Creator; if culture is the material, social, and symbolic matrix that results from the full range of mankind's creative activity; if culture cannot then be spiritually neutral or irrelevant, so that we can neither ignore it, nor withdraw from it, nor let it influence us uncritically, but must rather engage it responsibly; and if Christ is supreme as Lord of all; then Francis Schaeffer was right to insist that part of Christian discipleship is living out "the Lordship of Christ over the whole of life," which includes the totality of culture.[12] We have not understood adequately either the need for such living or the nature of what it asks of us.

When a more or less Judeo-Christian consensus was still dominant in American culture, it was easy

---

[12] "The Lordship of Christ over the whole of life means that there are no platonic areas in Christianity, no dichotomy or hierarchy between the body and the soul. . . . If Christianity is really true, then it involves the whole man, including his intellect and his creativeness." Francis A. Schaeffer, *Art and the Bible*, op. cit., 7, 9.

for Evangelicals to think of their faith as something that they practiced on Sunday morning. The rest of the week they did not really need to be that different from their neighbors — maybe a little bit more honest and moral, and if they were Fundamentalists, abstaining from alcohol, tobacco, and movies — but otherwise, not radically different. Becoming a Christian or "getting saved" was something they did as part of their religious life. There was no expectation that it would make much difference in how they ran their businesses, how they voted, how they raised their families, or — unless they were Fundamentalists — what kind of recreation and entertainment they would enjoy. Their approach was inconsistent: they were neither consistently withdrawing from culture nor effectively engaging it. Some of them practiced an incoherent hodgepodge of both strategies. Mostly, they were drifting with the culture, which was headed to places that would shock and dismay them a generation later.

Our Evangelical forebears made two mistakes which they have unfortunately bequeathed to many of us. First, they seriously overestimated how deep the Christian influence on American culture was. Traditional morality and the traditional family were in the 1950s being maintained out of habit, while any basis for those things in spiritual or even cultural commitment to their foundations was being hollowed out. Our failure to practice the Great Commission as it was given — to make *disciples* rather than merely converts — meant that the foundations of our Judeo-Christian culture were being undermined even while it looked like we were being successful in reaching people with the Gospel. Too many of our "converts" did not truly become born again, and hardly any of them were being taught the Christian worldview, much less sound doctrine.

The second mistake was a superficial understanding of the Lordship of Christ and its implications for all of life. Christian truth does not exist in an isolated, sealed chamber called "religion." It is true truth *about the world*, because God is the Creator of the world. Therefore Christ is Lord not just of my religion but of my *life*. No distinction can be made between "sacred" and "secular" realms of life that is not arbitrary. C.S. Lewis expressed the truth starkly but accurately: "There is no neutral ground in the universe; every square inch, every split second is claimed by God and counter-claimed by Satan."[13] As J. Gresham Machen put it, "The field of Christianity is the world. The Christian cannot be satisfied so long as any human activity is either opposed to Christianity or out of connection with Christianity."[14] If what the Bible teaches about God, man, and the world is true, it should make a difference in every area of life: how we relate to our family, to our fellow man, to work, to the state, to education, athletics, the arts — everything. Every area of private life, every arena of public life, must now be seen not as something existing autonomously on its own, but as something that exists in relation to Christ: to be redeemed by His grace, informed by His Word, brought into submission to His Lordship, and pursued for His glory. Most of our churches do not even make an effort to teach such things — which means they are making no effort to be disciple-making communities.

It is easy to miss the radical relevance of Christian truth to all of life because in many areas there is no difference *on the surface*. The solution to a mathematical equation is the same for a Christian,

---

[13] C.S. Lewis, "Christianity and Culture," in *Christian Reflections*, ed. Walter Hooper (Grand Rapids: Eerdmans, 1967), 33.

[14] Machen, *Education, Christianity, and the State*, 50.

a neopagan, and an atheist. The solution to which chemical formula of additives to my gasoline will make my car run smoothly and efficiently, or to which medicine will make my body do so, is the same whether I am a Christian, a Hindu, or a Muslim. The grammar by which I must construct my sentences to make them intelligible and the rhetorical flourishes by which I can arrange them to make them powerful are the same whether I am writing an evangelistic sermon, a promotion for Planned Parenthood, or a translation of *The Communist Manifesto*. There is no particularly "Christian" way of doing any of those things, or a host of other things. But that does not mean there is no difference as to *whether*, *how*, or *why* a Christian should do them.

Two plus two equal four. They do and must equal four and no other number, whatever your religious beliefs or philosophy of life. The Christian and the Non-Christian see the same truth — but they do not (or should not) see it the same way. The Non-Christian says, "Two plus two equal four. I have no idea why. It just seems to work. If I don't take account of this strangely stable fact when I try to balance my checkbook, I will get myself in a heap of trouble eventually, so I just accept it, and then never give it another thought. Whatever." The Christian should look at the same fact very differently: "Two plus two equal four. I can always trust this to be true. And it is thus an awe-inspiring example of the transcendent rationality and trustworthy covenant faithfulness of the beautiful mind of our glorious God, which reminds me to worship Him every time I balance my checkbook. Blessed be He!"

This is not just a matter of the Christian having access to an inspiring emotional penumbra around his facts when he wants it. Seeing all facts as God's facts always makes a practical difference too. Even when we do the same things as Non-Christians, we do them for different motives and with a different ultimate purpose in view. As a Christian I am not a private individual who has the option of making decisions solely to please myself. I am the servant of Another, bought with a price; I am the steward of the earth and the steward (not the owner) of all my own possessions; I am an Ambassador for Christ. Everything I do, and the way I do it, either advances or thwarts the objectives inherent in these identities. So I do not work just to make a living. I work to *serve* my employer and my neighbor *out of love*. The quality with which I do that is the context out of which my testimony for Christ flows. Martin Luther said somewhere that if you are a Christian cobbler, you accomplish all of this not by putting little crosses on your shoes, but by making really good shoes. A like mentality pervades my approach to every aspect of my life: as a husband or wife, a father or mother, a neighbor, an employee, an employer, a consumer, a citizen, a person just resting and relaxing, I must let my light so shine before men that they will see my good works and glorify my Father who is in heaven (Mat. 5:16). And I do it all not as a burdensome duty but as an expression of the joy of life, of gratitude for my redemption, and of love for God and my neighbor. There is not a single atom of reality or iota of truth about reality that comes into my field of vision that I do not see in relation to Christ.[15]

THESIS 5: THE CHRISTIAN SUBCULTURE IN ANY SOCIETY SHOULD BRING SALT AND LIGHT TO THAT SOCIETY THROUGH ITS OWN CULTURAL ACTIVITY, BOTH IN CREATING AND CONSUMING CULTURE.

Everything we do as Christians should reflect our identity as sub-creators, stewards,

---

[15] I spoke of this kind of seeing as "wholeness of vision" that flows from "biblical consciousness" in *Inklings of Reality: Essays toward a Christian Philosophy of Letters* (Lynchburg: Lantern Hollow Press, 2012). See that book for more practical advice on how to cultivate wholeness of vision and the Christian culture that should reflect it.

servants, and ambassadors of Christ. And because we are sub-creators, everything we do will make — or mar — culture, in one way or another. As homemakers, family members, gardeners, cooks, workers, voters, participators in social media, consumers of products, patrons of movies, books, music, and plays, members of clubs and of churches, and in a thousand other roles, we never cease to be both creators and consumers of culture. As people with a different set of beliefs which, however imperfectly, affect our sense of who we are, we will do it in our own unique way (or set of ways, since even the Christian subculture is not monolithic or uniform). Those different ways of life will get noticed as a subset of the larger culture which will interact with it in complex ways. American Christians will have their own ways of being Americans, for example; they are not going to live like First-Century Middle-Eastern peasants in the midst of American society. That all this will happen is inevitable. That we will do it well, or even deliberately, or thoughtfully, or intelligently, or faithfully to sound Christian teaching, is not.

Jesus uses two metaphors for His followers' presence in the world that describe the way they are supposed to relate to it and interact with it: salt and light. We are the salt of the earth, so we had better not lose our taste (Mat. 5:13). And we are the light of the world, so we had better not let ourselves be hidden away (Mat. 5:14-15) but rather be seen in such a way that our good works glorify the Father (Mat. 5:16). Salt was valued both as a preservative and as a flavoring. Light shows the path and shows up both good and evil for what they are (John 3:19-21). So the church's presence in the world should retard its natural slide toward corruption and evil, bring out and enhance the flavor of what is good in it, and keep the way toward grace and truth open and visible to people's eyes so that the Holy Spirit can call them into it.

We do this by preaching the Gospel and sharing our testimony, of course. We should also be doing it by showing the difference following Christ makes in our total way of life. We are still fallen people who sometimes stumble badly, but we should be stumbling on a new path in a new direction. (Remember that Christianity was first called simply "the Way.") That new path is marked by the new identity we have already been given in Christ (restored sub-creators, faithful stewards, heavenly ambassadors), and the new direction is toward the full incarnation of that identity that we will receive in its fullness and without compromise when we see Christ face to face. In the meantime, if our work manifests reliable quality for a fair price, if our homes manifest loving hierarchy without oppression, if our lives manifest creative applications of biblical principles that reveal goodness, truth, and beauty in many ways that can join with the heavens to declare the glory of God (Psalm 19:1), then our preaching of the Gospel will have a credibility and a power that we have not seen in our generation. Then the culture of the Kingdom of Heaven, reaching back into this present evil age in foretastes of the glory that is to come and finding ways to express itself in the idiom of the fallen cultures it invades, will be *seen*. And that may be the most convincing apologetic of all.

I have hesitated long over these next few paragraphs. I fear that I will not be able to write them so as to avoid some people charging me with elitism. And if elitism is what I am heard as preaching, I will have failed. Elitism lacks the divine humility that should characterize any genuine Christian culture. But bear with me if I sound elitist for the moment. I will try to redeem myself from that charge before the end.

I won't try to assess what kind of Christian subculture we have created in our homes, offices, or workshops. It no doubt ranges from splendid to abysmal, as one would expect. Others are better equipped to speak of those manifestations. Here I am thinking of the face we as Evangelicals and Fundamentalists present to the world with respect to that salient area of human creativity that is often mistakenly equated with culture: the arts. I am afraid it reflects the basic superficiality of our movement, which has often been described as a river a mile wide and an inch deep. What have we given to the world? Southern Gospel; "Praise and Worship;" the "Christian Romance Novel;" paintings of unrealistically pretty landscapes or Victorian villages with Bible verses tacked beneath them; cutesy figurines of angels who could not say, "Fear not!" with credibility if their wings depended on it.

There. I've just offended some of you. Forgive me, and hear me out. Not everything I just listed is always bad or inherently trashy. I like some Southern Gospel myself, when it stays close to its roots in folk music and the Negro spiritual. I don't think less of you if you do too. But nothing I just listed can pretend to be "high" or "serious" art. Why is that a problem? Why do we care if we are not nurturing a bunch of hoity-toity, snotty *artistes* who think they are better than everybody else? Because the very way I just framed that complaint loudly shouts of a prejudice against excellence that is absolutely foreign to, antithetical to, dismissive of, and loaded with antipathy towards our marching orders in Philippians 4:8. "Finally, brethren, whatever is true, whatever is honorable, whatever is pure, whatever is lovely, whatever is of good repute, if there is any exccllence, anything worthy of praise, dwell on these things." And I framed it in precisely the terms that would be on the lips of too many of us. We should not despise "low" or "pop" culture. I don't. Neither should we despise the high. As a whole, our movement does.

It has not always been this way. Conservative, Evangelical, Protestant piety once fostered the epics of Milton and Spenser, the devotional poetry of Donne and Herbert, the music of Bach and Handel.[16] Where is the American Evangelical author who writes anything that is, or can be, appreciated for its literary value by non-Christians who are not already biased in favor of its message? You can think of a few Christians in the Twentieth Century who achieved this feat without compromising their Christian content: G.K. Chesterton, C.S. Lewis, J.R.R. Tolkien,

---

[16] For a brilliant analysis of how specifically Protestant spirituality once fostered a rich literary culture, see Barbara Kiefer Lewalski, *Protestant Poetics and the Sixteenth-Century Religious Lyric* (Princeton: Princeton Uni. Pr., 1979). For further discussion of these matters, see my *Inklings of Reality: Essays toward a Christian Philosophy of Letters*, op. cit., esp. chap. 10, "Why Evangelicals Can't Write," 207-14.

Dorothy L. Sayers, and Flannery O'Connor. None of them were American Evangelicals. Why not? You get what you value as a community, as a subculture; you get what you encourage; you get what you reward. One of the reforms desperately needed if we are to give full witness to the Gospel with credibility is a healthier attitude toward culture in general and the arts in particular.

How do we get there? Not by despising pop culture; not by suddenly running out and trying to be artsier than thou; definitely not by copying the decadent art of the secular culture we live in. We don't want more cacophonic music in our worship services, more incomprehensible poetry in our libraries, or more ugly and chaotic paintings on our walls. We do it by reforming our attitude toward culture in the terms of these theses. We do it by teaching our children to appreciate the best that has been written, sung, and painted in the past and to value those artistic monuments for what made them great. We do it by teaching them that human culture has value because it flows from human creativity which flows from the image of God, and that, for those so gifted, it is a way of serving God that is cherished by our community. We do it by praying for them in those terms and supporting them with our attention and our dollars when they try. And then we may be astonished at the Renaissance, Reformation, and Revival that result.

This essay is excerpted from Williams's upcoming book, "Ninety-Five Theses for a New Reformation: A Roadmap for Post-Evangelical Christianity" (Semper Reformanda Publications, 2021).

Transhumanism and the Abolition of the Human Person

Julie Miller on Transhumanism's Materialistic Shortcomings

In its broadest sense, transhumanism is the view that humanity's problems can and should be solved through science and technology.[1] Humanity's chief problems, on this view, derive from our biological, cognitive, and psychological limits. Transhumanists, therefore, seek to overcome these limits through applying science and technology to human persons. And this, they propose, will eventually lead to a new species labeled "posthumans."[2]

Transhumanists envision a techno-utopia sometimes referred to as a triple 'S' civilization of

---

[1] Max More, "The Extropian Principles version 3.0, A Transhumanist Declaration," *MROB*, 1998, accessed March 15, 2020, https://mrob.com/pub/religion/extro_prin.html.

[2] Ibid.

superintelligence, superlongevity, and superhappiness, a future where there is a gradual blurring of the traditional boundaries between human persons and machines.[3] This transition is sometimes referred to as the Double Blur, or the two-pronged pursuit to build machines to be persons (then surpass humans), and at the same time to transform human persons into machines through artificial technological enhancements.[4]

Transhumanism's materialist philosophy of human persons fuels their ambition to merge humans with technology. They have a mechanistic picture of the world, where nature is modeled after a machine and human beings are part of that machinery. All natural objects are constituted of essentially the same kind of thing, namely fundamental particles in different configurations.[5] Transhumanist Nick Bostrom puts it this way, "If human beings are constituted of matter obeying the

---

[3] David Pearce, "What is Transhumanism? The 3 Supers," *Institute for Ethics and Emerging Technologies,* September 16, 2014, accessed March 15, 2020), https://ieet.org/IEET2/print/9543.

[4] Selmer Bringsjord and David A. Ferrucci, *What Robots Can and Can't Be* (Dordrecht, The Netherlands: Kluwer Academic Publishers, 1992), 4.

[5] Edward Feser, *Aristotle's Revenge: The Metaphysical Foundations of Physical and Biological Science* (Germany: editiones scholasticae, 2019), 46.

same laws of physics, then it should, in principle, be possible to learn to manipulate human nature the same way we manipulate external objects."[6] Transhumanists approach problems with a reverse engineering mentality. If something needs to be fixed, you take apart its components and determine the causal connections. If every problem can be converted into a technical problem, then the solution is simply the appropriate application of technology. Transhumanism reflects a strong commitment to carry to completion the materialistic metaphysical picture of reality to include human persons. In fact, if it were possible to merge humans with technology, meaning the entirety of body and brain were replaced with technology, it would count as evidence for the materialist philosophy of human persons.

Few would deny that the universe and natural objects are, in some respects, machine-like and that this point of view has resulted in many scientific achievements. However, this is only *part* of a complete explanation of reality, and it is legitimate to take exception when this materialist view is set up as the absolute and all-sufficient form of

---

[6] Nick Bostrom, "A History of Transhumanist Thought," *Journal of Evolution and Technology* 14, no. 1 (April 2005): 4.

explanation. I argue that transhumanism's materialist philosophy is inadequate to account for humanity's essential features, namely the existence of persons, enduring personal identity, ethics, values, individual autonomy, liberty, dignity, and rights. Because of their incomplete understanding of the human person, there is no reason to believe their proposed enhancements are metaphysically possible and, if attempted, would be good for human flourishing.

Materialism Cannot Account for the Existence of Persons

First of all, it is misleading for transhumanists to claim a strictly materialist explanation of human persons. Materialism denies the existence of persons in the ordinary sense, namely that we are substantial, conscious, rational, embodied selves with free will. Instead, they believe that human beings are the accidental products of a non-personal, purposeless, valueless evolutionary process driven by reproductive fitness. Nevertheless, because people generally hold the ordinary, commonsense view of themselves as substantial selves, transhumanists often employ "person" language in their writings in order not to appear extreme. Yet, this "person" language is inconsistent with their materialism and in the end, as I will show, transhumanists believe the concept of the person as illusory. They seem compelled to give an account of our commonsense assumptions — enduring identity, moral agency, individual autonomy, rights — but their explanations are incompatible with materialism. If they were intellectually honest, they would follow Francis Crick who candidly states the radical consequences of materialism:

> The Astonishing Hypothesis is that "You," your joys and your sorrows, your memories and your ambitions, your sense of identity and free will, are in fact no more than the behavior of a vast assembly of nerve cells and their associated molecules. As Lewis Carroll's Alice may have phrased it: "You're nothing but a pack of neurons." This hypothesis is so alien to the ideas of most people alive today that it can be truly called astonishing.[7]

Nothing undermines the materialist philosophy of human persons like the astonishing hypothesis that persons do not exist.

---

[7] Stewart Goetz and Charles Taliaferro, *Naturalism* (Grand Rapids: Wm. B. Eerdmans Publishing Co., 2008), 22.

Materialism Cannot Account for Enduring Personal Identity

Transhumanists claim that radical human enhancements are desirable because they are aimed at a person's well being. Practically speaking, if I am deciding whether to radically transform myself into a posthuman, it seems crucial to know that 'I' myself will experience this promised future existence. If the enhancements will not improve 'me,' then the rationale for deciding to enhance myself is less persuasive. Am I only creating my successor? In fact, transhumanism's materialist view of the human person and their patternist view of the self are not sufficient to account for personal identity that will persist throughout the trajectory of radical enhancements.[8]

According to transhumanism, the human person is best understood as a bundle of molecular and cellular complexes that can be engineered and manipulated.[9] For the transhumanist, the most

---

[8] Susan Schneider, "Future Minds: Transhumanism, Cognitive Enhancement and the Nature of Persons," *Neuroethics Publications*, July 1, 2008, accessed March 8, 2020, 1-14, https://repository.upenn.edu/cgi/viewcontent.cgi?article=1037&context=neuroethics_pubs

[9] Steven A. Hoffman, "Transhumanist Materialism: A Critique from Immunoneuropsychology," in Hava Tirosh-Samuelson and

important part of the bundle is the brain because a person's identity is encoded there in the form of a pattern of neural connections, memories, cognitive capacities, and sensory abilities. This core pattern changes very gradually in stages over time, yet it purportedly maintains continuity.[10] Ray Kurzweil's description of patternism affirms the gradual aspect of the changing pattern. He says, "I am rather like the pattern that water makes in a stream as it rushes past the rocks in its path. The actual molecules of water change every millisecond, but the pattern persists for hours or even years."[11]

Kurzweil analogizes the water with our biology and the pattern of the stream with our brain pattern. Yet, even if we grant that your brain pattern is you, this stream analogy has little to do with explaining

---

Kenneth L. Mossman, eds., *Building Better Humans? Refocusing the Debate on Transhumanism* (Frankfurt: Peter Lang, 2012), 275.

[10] Ray Kurzweil, *The Singularity is Near: When Humans Transcend Biology* (New York: Penguin Books, 2005), 258.

[11]Ibid., 383. Kurzweil's reference to the pattern in a stream is likely a nod to Heraclitus (c. 535-475 B.C.), who held that permanence is an illusion and change is the universal feature of reality. Plato and Aristotle both credit Heraclitus as saying, "It is impossible to step into the same water twice." See Plato, *Cratylus,* in Mortimer Adler, editor, *Great Books of the Western World, Volume 6* (Chicago: Encyclopedia Britannica Inc., 1990), 94; Aristotle, *Metaphysics*, in Mortimer Adler, editor, *Great Books of the Western World, Volume 7* (Chicago: Encyclopedia Britannica Inc. , 1990), 529 (1010a13).

how identity persists through radical enhancements. Water molecules in a stream change location by moving downstream, but never do they cease being water molecules. After all, transhumanists plan to replace every biological molecule with artificial technology. Additionally, Kurzweil admits the pattern is not permanent but persists only for a while. This is the first clue that he and other leading transhumanists are not ultimately concerned about the persistence of personal identity.

The project to merge humans with technology occurs in two phases. Phase one uses biotechnology, nanotechnology, cyborg engineering, and the Global Brain to replace our bodies and brains with non-biological parts. This phase is dependent on first being able to fully understand the intricate workings of biology. This obstacle is acknowledged by Ray Kurzweil, albeit as an afterthought to his optimistic claim: "Biology will never be able to match what we will be capable of engineering *once we fully understand biology's principles of operation*" (emphasis added).[12] Transhumanists are confident that by fully understanding biology and gene

---

[12] Kurzweil, *Singularity is Near*, 227.

expression, they will be able to manipulate the genome and thus enhance specific traits related to health, cognition, and emotions.[13] Thereafter, replacing these biological systems with artificial parts will proceed fairly easily. Our bodies and brains will be replaced with such things as synthetic DNA, artificial organs, artificial blood cells, cognitive nanobots, neural chips, neural implants, modified memory, artificial neurons and synapses, and brain/computer interfaces.[14]

With the phase one changes to brain patterns, it is unclear, on the patternist view of the self, how personal identity persists. Susan Schneider, who admits she is sympathetic toward transhumanism, finds this path from human to posthuman incompatible with the preservation of the original

---

13 This kind of reasoning is akin to "genetic determinism," which Philip Kitcher soundly refutes saying, "We do not live by our genes alone...Typically, many genes combine to affect the characteristics we observe, and their action can be perturbed by changes in the environment." Further, "It is possible that evolution fashioned the basic cognitive capacities—alles ubriges ist Menschenwerk, or everything else is manmade" (translation added). Philip Kitcher, Vaulting Ambition (Cambridge, Massachusetts: The MIT Press, 1990), 18, 19, 418.

14 Kurzweil, Singularity is Near, 257, 375. Cognitive enhancements through augmentation of thinking processes are typically described in terms of faster processing and increased access to immense quantities of data and information, not in terms of enhanced knowledge, understanding, and wisdom.

person's identity.[15] She likens transhumanism's enhancement trajectory to a "technophile's alluring path to suicide."[16] Further, phase one enhancements will blur the boundaries of the self because the body and brain will be merged with technology that is constantly connected to the internet, artificial general intelligence, and the Global Brain.[17] The enhanced self, merged with technology, will no longer have the sense of a single consciousness distinct from the external world. Our experience as autonomous individuals, the feeling of individuation and separateness, will seem fallacious when we are interacting every day with AGI and the collective Global Brain.

The loss of personal identity is not the only human cost of phase one enhancements; the inherent value of embodiment is also destroyed.

---

15 Susan Schneider, Artificial You: AI and the Future of Your Mind (Princeton: Princeton University Press, 2019), 89-91.

16 Ibid., 90.

17 Ben Goertzel, "Encouraging a Positive Transcension," Singularity Stewardship and the Global Brain Mindplex, 2004, accessed June 16, 2020, https://goertzel.org/dynapsyc/2004/PositiveTranscension.htm#_4._Singularity_Stewardship. Global Brain theory is the idea that the increasing interconnectedness of humans and computers produce a kind of distributed mind, collectively forming a higher level of intelligence. Goertzel expects that AGI would collect and synthesize the thoughts of all the people on the globe, add its own thoughts, then feed these ideas back to humans.

Phase one enhancements are meant to maintain the health of the body and brain long enough to be a 'bridge' to phase two technologies that are yet to be developed.[18] Kurzweil plans to achieve radical life extension through "a bridge to a bridge to a bridge."[19] Biotechnology is a bridge to nanotechnology which is a bridge to mind uploading. Thus, the body is only instrumentally valuable; it is used as the means to mind uploading, where one can then escape the body altogether.[20] Our self-understanding and experience affirm that we ought not treat our bodies in this way. Immanuel Kant's Principle of Humanity reflects this commonsense view of human dignity: "So act as to treat humanity, whether in thine own person or in that of any other, in every case as an end withal, never as a means only."[21] Transhumanism's materialist philosophy and utilitarian ethics make no room for the intrinsic value and dignity of embodied human persons.

---

[18] Kurzweil, *Singularity is Near*, 373.

[19] Ibid.

[20] Ibid., 371.

[21] Immanuel Kant, "The Metaphysics of Morals," *The Great Books of the Western World,* Volume 39, Mortimer J. Adler, ed. (Chicago: Encyclopedia Britannica, Inc., 1990), 272.

The aim of phase two enhancements, or mind uploading, is to transfer the biological brain to a more durable non-biological substrate.[22] Consider the following thought experiment: suppose the computational brain pattern of John is captured through Whole Brain Emulation (WBE), without destroying John's brain.[23] His pattern is then uploaded to a computer. On the patternist view, the same pattern means the same personal identity. Therefore, John and the upload on the computer are the same person. But this is obviously wrong. Even if we grant that an upload is a conscious person, it is not the very same person as the original John. The upload is a copy, not John himself. Only one person can be John. To make matters worse, the upload can be copied again and again.

---

[22] I have argued elsewhere that mind uploading is metaphysically impossible because transhsumanism's materialist philosophy of mind is false. Here, I demonstrate the human cost of pursuing these enhancement projects.

[23] Sim Bamford, "A Framework for Approaches to Transfer of a Mind's Substrate," *International Journal of Machine Consciousness* 4, no. 1 (2012), 23-34, accessed June 18, 2020, https://pdfs.semanticscholar.org/36cd/238588dee2b7fa36e

f2c3a0a80447b30b96a.pdf. Recent developments in the field of neural prosthetics has led to a method of WBE which would gradually replace all of the organic neurons of the brain with artificial synthetic parts.

This is an absurd view of the self with all kinds of ethical and legal ramifications. Ray Kurzweil defends the patternist view, with its absurdities, saying "It's not true that the [copy] is not you — it *is* you. It is just that there are now two of you. That's not so bad — if you think you're a good thing, then two of you is even better."[24] Likewise, Nick Bostrom applauds the potential advantages of mind uploading, such as "the ability to make back-up copies of oneself (favorably impacting on one's life-expectancy) and the ability to transmit oneself as information at the speed of light. Uploads might live either in virtual reality or directly in physical reality by controlling a robot proxy."[25]

Some transhumanists are more like Francis Crick and suggest the sense of self is an illusion. For instance, Ben Goertzel, Chairman of Humanity+, describes how the idea of personal identity will become obsolete in the future:

---

[24] Ray Kurzweil, *How to Create a Mind: The Secret of Human Thought Revealed* (New York: Penguin Books, 2013), 247.

[25] Nick Bostrom, "Transhumanist Values," Ethical Issues for the 21st Century, reprinted in *Review of Contemporary Philosophy* 4 (May 2005), 2, accessed November 12, 2019, https://nickbostrom.com/ethics/values.pdf .

Advances in technology will lead to the obsolescence of many of the most familiar features of our inner lives, like the way we conceive of ourselves, the feeling of free will that we have, the sense we have that our consciousness is sharply distinct from the world around us, the sense we have that our mind and awareness is within us rather than entwined in our interactions with other minds and the external environment.[26]

Similarly, James Hughes holds a Buddhist and Parfitian view of the self as an illusion.[27] He predicts that once technology gives us control of our memory, cognition, and personality, "we will abandon our Western view of individuality for new forms of collective identity."[28] Simply put, based on their own philosophy of patternism and the

---

[26] Ben Goertzel, "Artificial General Intelligence," in Max More and Natasha Vita-More, eds., *The Transhumanist Reader: Classical and Contemporary Essays on the Science, Technology, and Philosophy of the Human Future* (West Sussex, UK: John Wiley & Sons, 2013), 130-131.

[27] James Hughes, "Contradictions from the Enlightenment Roots of Transhumanism," *Journal of Medicine and Philosophy* 0 (2010): 1-19, accessed June 28, 2020, http://citeseerx.ist.psu.edu/viewdoc/download?doi=10.1.1.993.3636&rep=rep1&type=pdf.

[28] James Hughes, "The Future of Death: Cryonics and the Telos of Liberal individualism," *Journal of Evolution and Technology* 6, (July 2001), https://www.jetpress.org/volume6/Death.htm, accessed June 28, 2020.

admission of at least three transhumanist leaders, the self as a pattern will not survive gradual enhancements or mind uploading. In fact, on this scenario, the original self wills its own death. This outcome is paradoxical, especially since the primary motivation to become posthuman is to overcome death.[29] Clearly, transhumanists are more interested in using humanity as a means to create a new species of posthumans than preserving personal identity.

Materialism Cannot Account for Ethics, Values, and Duties

Transhumanist Max More maintains there is no agreement concerning a comprehensive transhumanist moral theory.[30] His claim seems to be an attempt to be consistent with transhumanism's materialistic evolutionary philosophy. As Michael Ruse acknowledges, "Ethics is an illusion put in place by natural selection to make us good cooperators."[31] However, despite

---

[29] Nick Bostrom, "Why I Want to be a Posthuman," in More and Vita-More, eds., *The Transhumanist Reader*, 33-35.

[30] Max More, "The Philosophy of Transhumanism," in More and Vita-More, eds., *The Transhumanist Reader,* 6.

[31] Michael Ruse, "The Biological Sciences Can Act as a Ground for Ethics," in Francisco Ayala and Robert Arp, Contemporary Debates in *Philosophy of Biology* (Oxford: Wiley-Blackwell, 2009), 1, accessed

transhumanists having no *formal* moral theory, it is not difficult to discover that they adhere to a set of values and a particular concept of human nature, namely a utilitarian ethic, the will to evolve and control human nature, and a belief in perpetual progress.[32] Yet, transhumanism's materialistic evolutionary philosophy offers no basis or framework for ethics, values, and duties.

A Utilitarian Ethic

In addressing ethical concerns, transhumanists typically hold to some form of utilitarianism.[33] Generally stated, the principle of utility tells us that right actions are those that have good consequences for the community. On this view, determining if a certain enhancement is morally right is based on whether there is a good outcome for society. For the transhumanist, a good outcome would be one that advances humanity's goal to transcend its biology.

July 15, 2020, http://philsci-archive.pitt.edu/4078/1/RusePhilSciArchive.pdf.

[32] Despite having no formal moral theory, transhumanists promote ethics on their most prominent websites: Humanity+ states its mission as "the ethical use of technology to expand human capacities," https://humanityplus.org/about/mission/ (accessed June 22, 2020). The online Transhumanist scholarly website is the Institute for Ethics and Emerging Technologies, which carries the label 'ethics' in its name, https://ieet.org/ (accessed June 22, 2020).

[33] More and Vita-More, eds., *The Transhumanist Reader*, 15.

For example, some biotechnologies will offer enhancements but require the willful destruction of thousands of human embryos.[34] The transhumanist perceives an enhancement as morally right based on the good consequences for the community, such as overall increased lifespan or cognition. The ends justify the means. Utilitarianism does not accord moral standing to individuals, such as human embryos. Even in cases where utilitarians acknowledge that individual rights do exist, these rights are not inherent or inalienable but contingent on whether they confer some advantage to society. In John Stuart Mill's well known work *Utilitarianism*, he expresses the contingent nature of individual rights which are grounded in utility.[35] In discussing justice, which he views as a sentiment, he writes, "All persons are deemed to have a right to equality of treatment, except when some recognised social expediency requires the reverse."[36] Likewise, transhumanists will abrogate individual rights

---

34 Brent Waters, *Human to Posthuman* (Burlington, VT: Ashgate Publishing Company, 2006), 48-9.

35 John Stuart Mill, "On the Connection between Justice and Utility," in *Utilitarianism* (London: Parker, Son, and Bourn, 1863), Hedweb.com, accessed August 15, 2020, https://www.utilitarianism.com/mill5.htm.

36 Ibid.

when it is decided those rights are no longer useful to society.

While self-described as having no formal moral theory, transhumanists still do not hesitate to use moral language such as 'ought' and 'should.' In the *Humanity+ FAQ* discussion of reproductive genetic engineering, transhumanists argue

> that parents have a moral responsibility to make use of these methods, assuming they are safe and effective. Just as it would be wrong for parents to fail in their duty to procure the best available medical care for their sick child, it would be wrong not to take reasonable precautions to ensure that a child-to-be will be as healthy as possible.[37]

Therefore, enhancing your offspring is seen not only as desirable, but as a moral obligation.

Values and Duties

The normative value shared by transhumanists is the will to evolve, a desire to transcend our biological limitations. In addition, the ability to

---

37 Humanity+ FAQ, "Why Transhumanists Advocate Human Enhancement as Ethical Rather than Pre-WWII Eugenics?" *Humanity+*, accessed June 23, 2020, https://humanityplus.org/philosophy/transhumanist-faq/.

manipulate the world is seen as a universal feature of being human.[38] Max More puts these two ideas together, "We will reshape our own nature in ways we deem desirable and valuable."[39] Simon Young describes it this way: "Human beings have an innate 'will to evolve,' an instinctive drive to expand our abilities in pursuit of ever-increasing survivability and well-being."[40] The desire for human enhancement and the ability to control nature are seen as universal, innate, and instinctive. Simon Young claims these desires are aimed at our well-being; they are good for their own sake. In Nick Bostrom's essay "Why I Want to be a Posthuman When I Grow Up," he argues that, for most current human beings, these posthuman modes of being will be very good for us.[41]

Transhumanists present their conception of human nature as normative, which is reflected in their dogmatism regarding their selected values. This brings to mind the Innovators in C.S. Lewis's

---

[38] Gregory Stock, "The Battle for the Future," in More and Vita-More, *The Transhumanist Reader*, 312.

[39] Max More, "The Philosophy of Transhumanism," in More and Vita-More, *The Transhumanist Reader*, 4.

[40] Simon Young, *Designer Evolution: A Transhumanist Manifesto* (New York: Prometheus Books, 2006), 19.

[41] Nick Bostrom, "Why I Want to be a Posthuman When I Grow Up," in More and Vita-More, eds., *The Transhumanist Reader*, 29.

The Abolition of Man, who debunk traditional values and virtues yet believe their own values are immune from the debunking process.[42] As philosopher Michael Hauskeller properly states, "It thus appears that [human] nature, after it has been expelled from the transhumanist paradise with a great show of indignation, is immediately invited back in through the backdoor, just as Lewis thought it would."[43]

Even if we grant that transhumanism's enhancements are for our good, we would need a standard by which to measure these changes. It seems rational that only enhancements that increase the well-being of our species would qualify as good. Using this standard, the trajectory of enhancements that ultimately reject and abolish the human species in order to evolve into a non-biological posthuman species should necessarily be judged as bad for human flourishing. The conclusion of Lewis is apt, "The rebellion of new ideologies against the *Tao* is a rebellion of the branches against the tree: if the rebels could succeed

---

[42] C.S. Lewis, *The Abolition of Man* (New York: HarperCollins, 2001), 29.

[43] Michael Hauskeller, "Prometheus Unbound: Transhumanist argument from (human) nature," *Ethical Perspectives* (March 2009), 11, *ResearchGate*, accessed March 2, 2020, https://www.researchgate.net/publication/232770169_Prometheus_unbound_Transhumanist_arguments_from_human_nature.

they would find that they had destroyed themselves."[44]

Regardless of transhumanism's commitment to a select set of values and ethics, their materialist evolutionary philosophy lacks the moral basis to support these values. That is, if matter is all there is and if human morality is the product of natural selection — meaning belief-formation is aimed at fitness and survival, not truth — then there can be no objective account of morality.[45] Hence, transhumanists have no grounds for believing their "select" moral knowledge and claims are true. If moral reasoning involves forming judgments about what one ought to do, those actions must be evaluated against an objective standard. If matter is all there is, there are no "ought" or"should" claims. In response to transhumanism's select values, Lewis would likely say,

> "I ought" is the same sort of statement as "I itch" or "I'm going to be sick." In real life when a man says "I ought" we may reply,

44 Lewis, *The Abolition of Man*, 44.

45 Mark D. Linville, "The Moral Argument," in William Lane Craig and J. P. Moreland, eds, *The Blackwell Companion to Natural Theology* (West Sussex, UK: Wiley-Blackwell Publishing, 2009), 391-417.

"Yes. You're right. That is what you ought to do," or else, "No. I think you're mistaken." but in a world of Naturalists . . . the only sensible reply would be, "Oh, are you?" All moral judgments would be statements about the speaker's feelings, mistaken by him for something else (the real moral quality of actions) which does not exist.[46]

Make no mistake, transhumanism's appeal to universal human values is not consistent with their commitment to a materialistic evolutionary philosophy. Therefore, there is no warrant to take their enhancement projects or their moral claims seriously.

Belief in Perpetual Progress

Another normative value promoted by transhumanists is perpetual progress. It is closely tied to the essential human characteristic of self-overcoming, or the will to evolve. In Max More's *Principles of Extropy 3.11,* perpetual progress is the number one value, defined as: "perpetually overcoming constraints on our progress and

---

46 C.S. Lewis, *Miracles* (New York: HarperCollins, 2009), 56, Electronic Edition. I maintain here that materialism and naturalism (as C. S. Lewis uses it) agree on an important feature: that reality is fundamentally impersonal and nonmental.

possibilities as individuals, as organizations, and as a species; growing in healthy directions without bound." [47] In Nick Bostrom's "Transhumanist Values," technological progress is a basic condition for the transhumanist project "to explore the posthuman realm." [48]

Philosopher George Santayana (1863-1952) argued against this kind of absolute change, saying, "Progress, far from consisting in change, depends on retentiveness. When change is absolute there remains no being to improve and no direction is set for possible improvement; and when experience is not retained, as among savages, infancy is perpetual. Those who cannot remember the past are condemned to repeat it."[49] If Santayana's reasoning is right, transhumanism's progress toward a posthuman species represents absolute change with no being, or self, left to improve.

---

[47] Max More, "Principles of Extropy 3.11 (2003)," *Lifeboat.com*, accessed June 23, 2020, https://lifeboat.com/ex/the.principles.of.extropy#:~:text=The%20P rinciples%20of%20Extropy%3A%20Version%203.11%20(2003)&t ext=Self%2DTransformation%3A%20Extropy%20means%20affirm ing,responsibility%2C%20proactivity%2C%20and%20experimenta tion.

[48] Bostrom, "Transhumanist Values."

[49] George Santayana, *The Life of Reason or The Phases of Human Progress* (New York: Charles Scribner's Sons, 1906), 284, quoted in Charles T. Rubin, *Eclipse of Man: Human Extinction and the Meaning of Progress* (New York: New Atlantis Books, 2014), 43.

Transhumanists rely on the doctrine of technological progress when promoting their triple 'S' techno-utopia. Whereas it is reasonable to assume that technology will continue to advance in the future, it is not reasonable to assume that it will impact moral progress. In fact, because there is no notion of purpose or end in materialistic science and technology, there is no basis for judging the value of the ends to be served by technology; that is, there is no basis for judging whether technological changes are improvements or not.

Transhumanists have complete confidence in technological progress which blinds them from realistically anticipating the human propensity for twisting good into evil. Accordingly, they generally dismiss humanity's potential for evil.[50] Consider the significance of the computer virus as a reflection of the human capacity for evil. The sole purpose of inventing a computer virus is to cause chaos and destroy. Ted Peters says, "There is something at work in the human mind that leads to the development of brute and unmitigated destruction. No increase in human intelligence or advance in

---

[50] Nick Bostrom is one transhumanist leader who addresses the global catastrophic risks of transhumanism in Nick Bostrom and Milan M. Cirkovic, eds., *Global Catastrophic Risks* (Oxford: Oxford University Press, 2008).

technology will alter this ever-lurking human proclivity."[51] The computer virus is an apt metaphor for the literal evil that could arise when we have software running in our brains and bodies and computers that control our nanobot immune system.[52]

This transhumanist blind spot is caused by three things: an overconfidence in technological progress, an assumption of human perfectibility, and a belief in a techno-utopia. As a remedy, I suggest a return to Christian Realism in the tradition of Reinhold Niebuhr (1892-1971). In the 1940's and 1950's, Niebuhr emphasized and exposed the sinful condition of human beings, a reality made undeniable because of World War I and II, Hitler, Stalin, the Holocaust, concentration camps, and the gulags. The Christian Realist would caution transhumanists against overestimating what can be achieved through technology apart from the gracious action of God. Niebuhr stressed that because of the human potential to choose evil and chaos, as well as what is good and fulfilling, progress

---

[51] Ted Peters, "Transhumanism and the Posthuman Future: Will Technological Progress Get Us There?" in Gregory R. Hansell and William Grassie, eds., *H+/- Transhumanism & Its Critics* (Philadelphia, PA: Metanexus Institute, 2011), 158.

[52] Kurzweil, *Singularity is Near,* 410-414.

is not inherently good, but ambiguous.[53] There is a need to acknowledge the human condition; the human potential to choose evil cannot be converted into a technological problem to be solved by enhancements. Only God can ultimately solve this problem.

Materialism Cannot Account for Individual Autonomy, Liberty, and Rights

Individual autonomy, liberty, and rights are promoted by transhumanists, especially the fundamental right to modify one's body and brain. They oppose government intervention and regulation as it relates to what they call the right to morphological freedom.[54] *The Transhumanist Declaration* states: "We favor morphological freedom — the right to modify and enhance one's body, cognition, and emotions. This freedom includes the right to use or not to use techniques and

---

[53] Reinhold Niebuhr, *The Nature and Destiny of Man,* 2 Volumes (New York: Charles Scribner's Sons, 1941-2), 2:240, quoted in Ted Peters, "Transhumanism and the Posthuman Future; Will Technological Progress

Get Us There?" In Gregory R. Hansell and William Grassie, editors, *H+/-: Transhumanism and Its Critics,* (Philadelphia: Metanexus Institute, 2011), 168.

[54] Anders Sandberg, "Morphological Freedom: Why We Not Just Want It, But Need It," in More and Vita-More, eds., *The Transhumanist Reader,* 60-1.

technologies to extend life, preserve the self through cryonics, uploading, and other means, and to choose further modifications and enhancements."[55]

Transhumanists defend the concept of cognitive liberty, defending the right of individuals to choose brain enhancements by applying biotechnology, neuropharmacology, machine interfaces, and collective neural networks.[56] It is the individual self that acts as a responsible agent and freely wills his own enhancement and self-transformation. The subject becomes the object of his own change. Anders Sandberg rightly says that morphological freedom is "the use of oneself as a tool to achieve oneself."[57] This echoes Lewis's warning in *The Abolition of Man* that "it is in Man's power to treat himself as a mere 'natural object' and his own judgements of value as raw material for scientific manipulations to alter at will."[58]

Despite the 'rights' language, transhumanism's materialist philosophy cannot account for the

---

[55] "The Transhumanist Declaration (2012)," in More and Vita-More, eds., *The Transhumanist Reader*, 54-5.

[56] Wrye Sententia, "Freedom by Design: Transhumanist Values and Cognitive Liberty," in More and Vita-More, eds., *The Transhumanist Reader*, 356.

[57] Sandberg, "Morphological Freedom," in More and Vita-More, editors., *The Transhumanist Reader*, 63.

[58] Lewis, *The Abolition of Man*, 72.

existence of the self as a free agent who has individual rights. In the early stages of their project, transhumanists use these concepts (as useful fictions) to appeal to people who hold a commonsense view of themselves. Transhumanists consistently portray the individual as a responsible agent of his actions. Because they appeal to individual autonomy and self-determination when defending the fundamental right to enhance, it appears that transhumanists are staunchly libertarian as it relates to free agency. Be that as it may, the concept of free human agency is problematic for the transhumanist as a materialist. If human persons are strictly physical, this entails that all mental events are caused by purely physical prior histories and, therefore, free actions are necessarily ruled out.[59]

In brief, transhumanists have no philosophical grounds for their appeal to individual autonomy

---

[59] David Papineau, "The Rise of Physicalism," 8, *Core.ac.uk.*, accessed April 14, 2020, https://core.ac.uk/download/pdf/74162.pdf . The Causal Closure Argument for Materialism:

Conscious mental occurrences have physical effects.

All physical effects are fully caused by purely physical prior histories.

The physical effects of conscious causes aren't always overdetermined by distinct causes.

and free will in defending the right to enhance. The inadequacy of their materialist philosophy to account for individual autonomy and liberty is one of the reasons there is a blatant inconsistency between defending individual autonomy and upholding their utilitarian ethic. Utilitarian David Pearce abrogates individual liberty in favor of the authoritarian state when discussing the challenges of a future techno-utopia that has overcome death.

> Control of human reproduction, whether sexual or clonal, will be a generic feature of any post-aging civilization. The need for social mechanisms of reproductive control on pain of Malthusian catastrophe isn't a specific peculiarity of the abolitionist project. If (post)humans aren't going to grow old and die, as we do today, then we can't go on having children at will indefinitely. A regime based on genetic Russian roulette will be replaced by an ethically responsible policy of planned parenthood.[60]

---

[60] David Pearce, "Chapter 4, Objections 4.31," in *The Hedonistic Imperative, HedWeb.com*, accessed June 15, 2020, https://www.hedweb.com/hedethic/hedon4.htm#natural.

Transhumanists also express inconsistencies between their belief in individual self-determination and their belief that free people are often mistaken about their own best interests. Despite favoring liberal views of individual autonomy in their promotion of transhumanism, few believe democracy will be the final and best form of government for a future techno-utopia.[61] Their rationale for authoritarianism is that knowledgeable rulers understand the needs of the people better than the people themselves.

Transhumanism's reason for envisioning a technocratic authoritarianism is that a superior posthuman would know better what people need. Nick Bostrom calls for a global "singleton" to mitigate existential risks inherent in emerging technologies. He defines the singleton as "a world order in which there is a single decision-making agency at the highest level."[62] The singleton could be

[61] James Hughes, "Contradictions from the Enlightenment Roots of Transhumanism," Journal of Medicine and Philosophy (2010), 8, accessed June 25, 2020, http://citeseerx.ist.psu.edu/viewdoc/download?doi=10.1.1.993.3636&rep=rep1&type=pdf.

[62] Nick Bostrom, "What is a Singleton?" *Linguistic and Philosophical Investigations*, Vol. 5, No. 2 (2006), 48, accessed June 25, 2020, https://www.nickbostrom.com/fut/singleton.html.

a democratic world republic, a world dictatorship, a friendly superintelligent machine, or a posthuman.[63] Its purpose would be to solve global problems that might result from new dangerous technologies, like nanotechnology. "The singleton could relieve inequalities and suppress wars with help from improved surveillance, mind-control technologies, and communication technologies."[64]

In the end, transhumanists have no philosophical grounds for appealing to individual autonomy and free will in defending the right to enhance. In fact, when these concepts are no longer useful to the future society, they likely will disintegrate in the face of a technocratic authoritarian rule. Again, it turns out Lewis was right:

> It is in Man's power to treat himself as a mere 'natural object' and his own judgements of value as raw material for scientific manipulation to alter at will. The objection to his doing so does not lie in the fact that this point of view (like one's first day in a dissecting room) is painful and shocking till we grow used to it. The pain and shock are at most a warning and

---

[63] Bostrom, "What is a Singleton?" 48.

[64] Ibid., 52.

a symptom. The real objection is that if man chooses to treat himself as raw material, raw material he will be: not raw material to be manipulated, as he fondly imagined, by himself, but by mere appetite, that is, mere Nature, in the person of his de-humanized Conditioners.[65]

Conclusion

My critique demonstrates that the transhumanist cannot adequately account for the human person based on their materialist, mechanistic, reductionist metaphysics. The essential features of humanity that materialism leaves out — the substantial self, enduring identity, morality, free will, inherent dignity, and rights — are the very things that a philosophy of human persons needs to explain and a technology that proposes to enhance human persons must account for. Since their materialist philosophy offers such an incomplete understanding of the human person, there is no justification for believing their proposed trajectory of enhancements are metaphysically possible and, if attempted, would be good for human flourishing.

---

[65] Lewis, *The Abolition of Man*, 72-3.

Stained-glass Man

Donald W. Catchings, Jr. on
Man's Own Image

I

Once upon a time, there was a Stained-glass Man
Who held a glass world in the palm of his hand.
Day in and day out, the Man caught the eye
Of each and every passerby.

In rain and in shine, in snow and in heat,
Stained-glass Man stood, with pilgrims at his feet,
Giving hope to the sick and joy to the old;
He was even known to humble the bold.

With an unending love, his glass smiled upon
The rich and the poor, the old and the young —
Those cascading hues of turquoise and blue,
Budding with lilies and rose bushes, too.

White-robed, transfigured in heralded beauty,
Stained-glass Man shone, refracting Light's purity.

Shining the mark for wanderers to find
What they had been seeking all of their life.

Unchanged by time, with stained-glass mercies,
The Man welcomed all who came broken and
hurting.
Year in and year out, raised high above,
Over arched doors, He led all to love.

In war and in peace, for friend and for foe,
Steady, yet fragile, guiding all who would go
Making amends with foes and with friends;
He bore redemption in his stained hands.

With an inviting breadth, his arms opened wide
Calling to pauper and prince, "Come inside!
Here you will find the Word that gives life.
Here you will find He who bore strife.
Here you will learn what it means to be man.
Here you will finally come to understand
Why quintessence of dust was shaped and molded,
Why Maker, from clay, with His own hand promoted
An image like His; and what that image was:
Eternal, beautiful — made to love."

II

Once upon a time there was a man made of straw,
With mouth full of chaff — confusion, his drawl.
Day in and day out he would glare and cry
For he wished to pass Stained-glass Man by.

Neither rain nor shine, neither cold nor heat
Could straighten his back or sturdy his feet.
He hung — bitter, dejected — longing for something.
No. No. No. No. It was nothing. Yes, nothing.

With back-prodding pang, unrelenting and crude,
Straw-man stayed hanging while his heart rued
The day he was stuffed with his hollow life:
The day he began to grow weary of strife.

Month followed month and year followed year,
No pleasure could bring a morsel of cheer
For more than an hour or even a minute —
Straw-man's chest weaker than the fodder within it.

Poor wretched straw, watching seconds click on.
Deriding the minutes, the summers, the falls.
Perched among lilies, spurning their beauty;
Longing for love . . . longing so purely.

Robed in the shadows, rejecting all colors,
Save for the one trusted to blot out all others —
Blacker than pitch. No sun-shining grace
Could wipe the scowl from his burlapped face.

As life turned to death, Straw-man hung alone
In a field left unharvested, and not even sown.
Still, murders of doubt came pecking and pricking:
Those crows of confusion kept tearing and ripping.

After years of staring at Stained-glass Man's beauty,
Straw-man at last snapped that foul nail protruding
From the stake at his back, then fell to the ground
With a soft thud. He arose, turning himself round.

Once Straw-man came down from secluded perch,
He stumbled and hobbled, then bumbled and
    lurched.
While leaned on the post, taking in a new strength,
Straw-man looked up and thought on at length:

He thought about how he'd been left to himself,
While scores of travelers beheld someone else;
He thought about how that Stained-glass man stood,
Steady and true, so beautiful and good.

With rancor in heart and greed-strengthened feet,
Straw-man pressed on, his mind set to meet
A Stained-glass man, whose presence was mocking,
A Stained-glass man, so certain and haughty.

The day finally came; He passed Stained-glass man,
With mouth full of hate and foul rock in his hand.
With burning lips, Straw-man raised clenched fists;
He had to say something — this moment was his.

Today was the day, final straw, the last time
As Stained-glass Man caught this straw-man's eye
He reared back and let his foul rock flash,
Cursing the heavens as his rock smashed:
"Who said you were beautiful, good, or true?
What gives you the right to speak for me, too?
How dare you stand proud, day in and day out,
Passing your judgment on innocent crowds?
You're nothing but glass, fashioned to shine
On poor scores of fools too lost in the rind
To see for themselves what they really need,
To see your invite as a gesture of greed,
To know they can fashion, solicit, promote
Themselves as they please, prefer, and want.
That is true love — the real image of man,
To hold his own world in the palm of his hand."

III

Thus Straw-man gave his shattered speech,
<u>Broken like the glass scattered at his feet:</u>

"Look. There lies that Stained man.
Pfft . . . **His** glass is smashed.
Pick **Him** up; **He**'ll cut your hand.
Once upon a time, pilgrims passed
To be guided to *goodness* and *sureness of mercies.*
Now, AT LAST!
His mercy —
broken.
His guidance? —
It's gone.
Reds, whites, and blues. In various hues.
He'll cut your feet to pieces.
That's who **He** really is (The purpose of **His** image)
Come one! Come all! TAKE
As you will...
Drink, ***His*** *wine*? Eat, ***His*** *cake*?
(No longer)
No need to buy
Or sell. That's what **His** book says!
I say — Have your fill. Take what.
What you. What <u>you</u> will.
Will. Have your fill. Take!"

<u>Then, the crowds rushed in</u>:

"I saw it first. Give that to me."
"No! That one's mine. I'll take what I want."
". . . Take it! I dare you!"
"I will. Try and stop . . ."

Each stole a piece from the ground
Or tore it from another's hand.
(Blood everywhere) As a souvenir.
(Spitting. Kicking. Cursing.)
To call it their truth and sneer:

"Now, that is what beauty is."
"Aw. Yes. This is good."
     "Just a piece, a fragment . . .
good enough."
"All of Him was too much."
"I'll take this shard . . ."
"I . . . this one."
"Me. This is the perfect piece."
"I can make it . . ."
"I can make Him what . . ."
". . . I want."

Nevertheless, when the crowds
were gone

There were just as many pieces left
As there were when the chaos
had begun.
For no matter how many pieces were taken,
There was still more to give —
Even in shards, Stained-glass Man still would
give of himself.
Thus, Straw-man decided to do the gravest
thing (he decided to do his worst)
gluing Stained-glass Man back together.
Hours in and hours out
(Blood. Sweat. And Tears) Heap of broken glass.
Mingling death, spit, glue.
Mangling reds, whites, blues.
Slowly, it turned to something else.
Something grotesque.
Goya would be nauseated.
(de Kooning would be creeped out)

Once Straw-man was done gluing his foul artwork,
He perched on his soapbox and gave
his final word —

IV

Ecce Homo
There He stands:

Spit in His beard;
Blood in his eyes.

Ecce Homo
There He stands:
Robed in mockery —
Beaten; Humble; Alone.

Ecce Homo
There He stands:
A man? Yes, a new man.
The Man whose image
All men have made . . .
Straw-man has made.

Behold the Man:
Broken?
Fixed?
Is.
Whoever I am.
Whatever you desire.

V

Once upon a time, there *was*.

My Favorite Things

Christy Luis on Coming Out of
and Into the Fire

Ash fell like snow on the black walnut tree across the street.

Diana peered at it through the kitchen window, but swirling smoke obscured her view. She imagined the ash into snowflakes.

"Silver white winters that melt into springs," she sang softly. She imagined her father's nine-hundred square foot apartment into Nonnberg Abbey without any trouble and --

A knock on the door startled her from her daydream of Salzburg, Austria.

Almost without thought, she began rolling her wheelchair toward her bedroom. *How did I miss the sound of his car?* She pictured her father bursting into the apartment as she fled.

But . . . her father wouldn't knock, she realized. She stopped rolling the chair and tried to imagine who might brave the ash and smoke for a visit.

The evacuation orders had only been lifted a few hours before.

In the apartment's single bedroom, she could hear blankets swishing and the floor creaking. Moments later, her sister Kari appeared at the bedroom door with a bad case of helmet hair.

"It's just some cult Bible thumper," she announced in a scratchy, overloud voice. "Useless nuts can't even let the firefighters SLEEP."

Kari had been working overtime to fight the wildfires roaring through northern California. Sometime in the last decade, the period from late spring to late fall had become known as "fire season." Kari often had to work ridiculous overtime hours that left her staggering with exhaustion. Several times, she had been forced to sleep at one of the fire shelters with Di, as their own home was evacuated. They had been staying in a fire shelter for the last four nights.

After working an extra 24 hour shift, Kari had stumbled into the shelter around 2 A.M. that morning. When the shelter announced that the mandatory evacuations had been lifted, Kari drove them back home.

Ever since they got home, Kari had been sleeping, but she clearly still hadn't recovered.

Di could sympathize with her sister's grumpiness, but she wouldn't have minded talking with the visitor. "It is an awkward time to visit people," she ventured, "but they must be pretty devoted."

She then turned back to the electric stove and dumped a bowl of scrambled eggs into a frying pan. Impatiently, she turned the heat on high.

"Are they gone, yet?" Kari groused. "I need more sleep before my next shift."

Di rose slowly from her wheelchair so she could press her cheek against the glass of the kitchen window. A shadowy figure was retreating from the front step.

"Yeah. But they left something on the doormat."

Kari retrieved the whatever-it-was. "It's the solicitor's book!"

Di rolled the wheelchair over to look. The book was thick and had a cracked leather cover that read "Holy Bible."

The smell of burning eggs suddenly filled the room, making Di gag ferociously. She had to eat eggs every day, often twice a day, as they were a cheap and easy protein; as a result, she could barely stomach burned eggs anymore.

A person could only eat so many scrambled eggs, she felt.

"I wish people would leave us alone," Kari muttered blearily. "We take care of ourselves, if nobody bothers us."

Di always warmed inside when Kari referred to "us." She knew she was the exception to Kari's generally hostile outlook on humanity. At the same time . . . she wished her sister were a bit more friendly with the rest of the world. They didn't *actually* support themselves very well.

She leaned over one arm of her chair and rummaged through the fast food bags scattered on the floor. "Can we go to McDonald's?"

"Yeah, I know we need more ketchup. But not if we're out of eggs, right?" Kari sighed. "I'll soak some beans and pick up pears from the food bank. We need to stretch a few more meals out of this paycheck . . . "

A car rumbled into the apartment's parking lot, then fell silent. A door slammed.

Kari didn't react, busy with her thoughts; but Di's mindset shifted instantly. She shoved her eggs into her mouth until she choked.

"Swallow," she ordered herself. But she couldn't fight her heightened gag reflex and spat the mess back onto her plate. She threw it in the sink just as Kari exploded into a tirade.

"If only he didn't spend it all on drugs!"

"Mmhm."

"But those cops just won't take him! It's like, what does a guy have to do to get arrested in California? Does he have to murder you first? Do his kids have to die of neglect?"

Kari continued airing her favorite complaints, and Di ignored her as she wheeled herself down the hall to their shared room. Finally, she shut the door on her sister's stream of chatter.

Just in time. The front door creaked and slammed.

A second later, her father's voice boomed through the house. "Smells like burnt egg in here. Did Gimpy waste our last eggs?"

His footsteps creaked toward the kitchen.

Kari's voice settings were still on "shout." "Diana has been taking care of herself *again*, so don't blame her! Speaking of which, she'll have to skip school on Monday and Tuesday. Her wheelchair-"

"Would you shut up about that wheelchair?"

"-- is so small that she developed *another* pressure sore. Now she has to homeschool until it heals."

Di quietly rolled her wheelchair into the corner of the room, past her sister's mattress to lie down on her own mattress. She lay on her side to avoid her tailbone's pressure sore. She hadn't even felt the ulcer, since it was below her lumbar vertebrae; Kari had noticed it when helping Di undress for a bath at the emergency fire shelter, two nights before. They had practiced the bath-check ritual every week since she was born with spina bifida.

She could usually sit up for about two hours before she needed to lie down and let the throbbing sore rest. In a few days, it would heal enough to let her attend half days at school; but her sister and father would both be working — Kari on 48 hour shifts and her father on a construction job hours away. So she would be stuck at home until she could stand to attend full days.

Di didn't really care. Her teachers had already handed out schedules and Chromebooks in case of evacuations, so she could work if she wanted to. But she didn't want to. She was tired of working so hard at everything.

Outside of her room, the discussion continued. "Why don't *you* buy her a new chair, Kari?"

"Sure, with all my extra money."

"Oh yes . . . that's right. You don't have any money, do you? Because you got fired."

Di gasped.

"No I didn't!"

"Are you or are you not currently *volunteering* at the fire department?"

". . . Yes. The department laid me off two weeks ago. The county cut funds, so the department only has money to keep two firemen on staff at a time. But I'm applying at the tree service!"

"You should be job hunting all day, Kari. Not sucking up to the department that laid you off."

"It won't last," Kari said in a soft voice. "They'll take us back. I know they will . . . and right now, they need my help whether they can pay me or not."

Oh no.

"But until you get hired . . . you'll be staying somewhere else."

"You're *kicking me out*?"

"If you can't pay for your share, you're not living here."

"Who are you going to share rent with?"

"I have friends. Get out."

"... I have to pack. I'll leave in the morning." Kari entered their bedroom. Her eyes shone strangely bright in the dim light.

"Diana." She spoke with restrained intensity. "I swear, I won't leave you alone with him." She sank onto her own mattress. "I have a plan. I can't tell you what it is, right now, but ... I have a boyfriend."

"You do?"

Kari didn't even look embarrassed about this secret.

"I started dating a cop, Officer Brantley. And I've been saving up. It's not enough for a new place, but . . . just trust me. It'll grow. It'll grow fast, and then you can live with us."

Di let her mind wander back to the events of the last week, when the mandatory evacuation was announced. She had carried her chair downstairs by herself, on numb legs, and called several people before finding a ride to the high school shelter.

She closed her eyes. "Don't worry about me, Kari. I escaped the fire on my own, remember? I can avoid Dad."

* * *

Di lay still until Kari slept, dreaming of life in Nonnberg Abbey. She never dreamed of living with Captain von Trapp and his seven children; it was the peaceful abbey that called to her.

Kari had set the black Bible on the floor, and Di picked it up. Immediately, her abbey daydream came to her.

Inside the abbey, everybody would treat each other kindly. Each morning, they chorused praises and prayers. They split the chores: fishing the lakes for breakfast, fetching firewood for the dining room's wrought iron grates. In the afternoon, Di would practice with the choir.

Resurfacing from her dream abbey, Di thought Kari's breathing sounded deep and regular. She rose from bed and crept into the living room, placing her crutches carefully to avoid the creaky spots.

A cocktail of smoke scented the air. What would the air quality index have said about the air inside their apartment? More or less hazardous than the wildfire smoke outside?

Her father snored on the couch, TV light flashing against his face. A glowing blunt dangled from two of his fingers, very nearly resting on his furry chest.

His stomach caved in at an unhealthy slant before the rest of his body disappeared beneath a blanket. Her father teased her for being "chunky," but she felt healthier than he looked.

How could he function well enough to work construction?

The answer lay on the table beside him — a bag of brownish crystals beside a glass pipe with a bulbous end. On weekends, like today, he sought a different kind of high.

Carefully, Di plucked the blunt from his grasp and dropped it onto the floor, a meter from his feet. It could have easily rolled there all on its own . . . and it settled against his chemical-laden work clothes, which began to smoke.

She returned to her room.

A new kind of smoke — *mm, burning carpet* — was just reaching her nose as she lowered herself silently onto her mattress, heart pounding. Waiting.

Kari's firefighter nose woke her quickly and she sat up. "The smoke smells stronger. I hear it. It's — oh! Jump out the window, Di!" Kari threw the window open and began tossing items through it: her cell phone, her purse, Di's pill case, and loose medication bottles.

Di opened the door to the living room and saw that her father's blanket was on fire.

"DAD! WAKE UP!"

He started awake, staring at her.

"YOU'RE ON FIRE!"

He roared and leapt to his feet. She hobbled back into the bedroom and grabbed her books from the bed stand. As she stuck one leg out the window, her father burst out the front door. Di might have laughed as he ran past, buck naked, except that one of his socks was on fire.

He dove head first over the railing into the yard below, trying to tear off his sock without burning his hands.

Di felt as though she were falling, and landing, winded, along with him. Her vision whitened, and she wobbled on the windowsill. She held her breath, willing herself to climb down, but she couldn't stop shaking. Finally, Kari helped her out.

As Di knelt on all fours, coughing and crying, Kari called the fire department.

* * *

Di and Kari crossed the street, away from their low-income apartment. Their father lay on the ground, running water from the spigot over his burned foot.

"I think I sprained my ankle climbing out," Kari said. She was rubbing one giant, muscular calf through weed leaf-print leggings. "You could have given me a little warning!"

"What do you mean?"

"Stop pretending. I heard you come from the living room. You started the fire."

Di looked at her feet and noticed, for the first time, that her own socks were soaked. She couldn't feel the wetness, but she felt cold all over.

"And it would have been a good idea, if we had renter's insurance," Kari continued.

Di winced.

"But even if we did, you still should have warned me first. I'd have done it for you."

Di remained silent for a long minute. "I knew you would say that."

"Of course you did. Don't I always take care of you?"

"I want to take care of us, for once."

Suddenly, something smashed into Di's back. With a cry, she crawled away to protect her tailbone.

Behind her, Kari swore. "You're going to make her bleed again, you meth-mouthed moron! She saved your life!" Under her breath, she muttered, "More than I'd have done."

Di turned around to find her dad's face inches from hers.

"You did this," he growled at her, leaning in close enough that clumps of his long, greasy hair brushed her nose. She thought she could feel it leaving a residue on her carefully scrubbed skin. His breath smelled strongly of marijuana and made her start coughing again. "I saw you walking out of the living room. Just wait until I get you alone, Gimp."

He walked away, swearing, because people were flocking out of the apartments in response to the smoke detectors. Kari started to follow him, but Di called her back.

"Don't break his face. You need a job, not a felony charge."

Kari didn't smile. "I won't let him hurt you again."

"Don't worry. The cops will take me away from him."

"What?"

"I'll tell them he fell asleep smoking, and his cigarette must have set the fire."

"No!" Kari jumped as fire sirens sounded in the distance. "You leave the talking to me. You were asleep and saw nothing. Okay? If we're lucky, the cops will take him on a meth charge. I nabbed some of it from his stash, earlier." She brushed Di's cheek with the back of her hand. "Let me mastermind this."

* * *

An hour later, Di sat in a police detective's car, wrapped in a blanket. The detective had left the door open, so neighbors and strangers stared at her.

The detectives directed most of their questions at Kari and their father. Eventually, one brought her a cup of tea to warm her hands.

"Hi, Diana," he said with a smile. "I'm Detective Bounds. I have a daughter near your age."

"Could you use a spare?"

"Excuse me?"

Di gestured to the smoldering ruins of her apartment. "I'm homeless. Happy to have a new home."

He laughed, and Di smiled, but secretly she wanted to just hop into his car and hide from the world — especially her father.

"I have a few questions for you." The detective opened a miniature flip pad. "When did you smell the smoke?"

"When my sister woke me up."

"Are you sure you weren't already awake?"

"We were both asleep," Kari called from nearby, where a separate cop had been questioning her. "You can talk to me."

Di suspected that the detective's notebook already contained many pages worth of information from Kari, but he nodded politely.

"Mr. Coburn says Diana was still awake when he drifted off."

"My father smokes meth, sir. He should be in prison. I wouldn't trust his word over Di's. She's practically a saint."

"Mmhm," he replied, glancing at Di again. "Well, girls, medical here says your father only sustained minor burns. The hospital will probably release him in a few hours, and he'll join you wherever you're staying."

"So he's not going to jail?" Di clarified.

"No. We found his meth pipe, and your sister gave us the meth, but that charge won't keep him in jail."

"And Di still has to live with him?" Kari demanded.

"We called Di's social worker, and she promised to visit next week."

The detective leaned against his car, as if to shield Di from his inevitable words. "But yes," he said, directing his comment back to Di.

"I . . . think Child Welfare Services will want to keep you with him. California likes to keep kids with their parents."

Di looked past the detective and met her father's red-eyed stare. The emergency medical technicians were still strapping him to the gurney to take him to the hospital.

"Officer," Kari complained, "our father is so wasted, he can't even see this was his fault. He was actually *threatening* Di just before you got here-"

"NO! N-n-no he wasn't." Di nearly choked on the lie. "He was just worried."

Kari sighed through her nose, glancing at Di's expression.

"Diana set the fire," her father shouted, making one of the EMTs wince. "I saw her do it!"

"He's lying!" said Kari. "Don't you think I'd have woken up if my little sister was tottering around on her crutches?"

The cops separated the family members, and Di ended up back in the apartment's parking lot with Detective Bounds. Most of the building appeared undamaged, except for their unit and the rooms belonging to their neighbors.

"Listen, Diana," the detective told her. "I have eyes. I know your father isn't taking care of you, and I know you're probably angry about that. I also know that you probably still love him." He sighed. "I worked in the juvenile division before I became a PD and I still see this stuff all the time. It makes me sick. But I just want you to know . . . if you did set that fire, you shouldn't try it again. Don't do it. It'll just get you sent to a juvenile hall somewhere out of county. It's a pain. You and I know that you didn't mean to hurt him; you just wanted him in jail. I sympathize — because he definitely belongs in jail. But others won't see it that way, when they review your case. Now let's get some breakfast, and I'll bring you wherever your sister and father are staying."

Breakfast, Di thought with a sigh. *I couldn't care less about breakfast. I just want to be somewhere, anywhere else.*

She thought about what he said, as she rode with him to the only diner in town that was open at this hour. It took less than a car ride to dismiss his words as irrelevant. He was basically saying, "It sucks, but there's nothing either of us can do about it." And that just wouldn't work for her.

* * *

They ended up in a shoddy trailer provided by Kari's boyfriend. Di and Kari watched television from sleeping bags on the floor.

Their father snored nearby on the only bed. After taking him home from the hospital, Kari had plied him with alcohol against the strict prohibition of the burn unit doctor. Eventually, he'd fallen into a fitful sleep, just as dawn light began filtering through the windows.

Kari had rolled a blunt from his stash. The hits barely affected her, and Di wondered how often her sister smoked and partied. Kari kept her life private from Di — even, apparently, that she dated cops.

After Detective Bounds left, the cop who had spoken with Kari earlier introduced himself as

Officer Brantley, "Kari's boyfriend," and invited the family to stay in his backyard trailer.

But the three of them couldn't stay in his trailer forever. Kari would leave Di alone with their father *eventually*.

Di tried retreating to Nonnberg Abbey, which had always welcomed her home. Tonight, it looked hazy when she struggled to visualize it.

She eyed the Bible, which made a distinctive dent in her trash bag full of scavenged belongings. The heavy book kept drawing her attention . . .

Someone had cared enough to bring it to her in the midst of the evacuations.

She pulled it from the bag and hugged it to her chest. Finally, the abbey rose in her mind *and she walked up the hill toward the gate.*

But she smelled smoke, instead of the usual garden and fresh night air. She followed a thick trail of smoke toward the great wooden door of St. John's Chapel.

Nuns silently huddled in the glow from the open doors. She pushed past them, despite the deafening roar and crackle of the fire. But she couldn't see. She coughed, as she breathed in the ash of aged artifacts and wonders.

She ran into the chapel . . . and woke up in Officer Brantley's trailer. She lay very still, trying to interpret and think her way out of panic.

Eventually, she stood again and began to gather tools: the smoldering blunt, a bottle of tequila from the dresser, and a pile of clothing from the floor.

Before she finished, Kari's phone screen lit up beside the ashtray, and Di froze until it went dark again.

Finally, she brought her tools into the tiny trailer's tiny bathroom and had to stand over the toilet to shut and lock the door after her. A shower stall stood beside the toilet.

She sat on the toilet seat, lay the clothes on the floor, and poured tequila on the pile.

"God?" she whispered. "I'm sorry about this. But it can't be worse for my soul than arson, and I won't let him kill me."

She took a long draw from the blunt, just as someone knocked on the door. "Di? Why are you talking?"

"Um . . . praying."

"Why? Di open this door *right now*."

Di took another quick drag on the blunt, then shook some glowing ash onto a thin t-shirt. It immediately lit with a blue flame, and she set the blunt on the tequila-soaked clothing.

"I'm fine, Kari. I'm just smoking."

"I'm going to break down the door."

As the bathroom grew hazy, Di inhaled the scent of marijuana. Lots of people had died this way in the California fires. Maybe if she burned out all the bad, she would wake up in the abbey. The nuns would welcome her . . . they would understand.

I'll just wait for the fumes--

The bathroom door burst open, landing at a slant on top of her head. Her teeth clacked together and her head suddenly felt too heavy for her neck.

The door pulled away as quickly as it had fallen on her, and Kari jumped inside. She was crying, as she tossed the burning clothes into the shower stall.

"Did the door hurt you? *Are you okay*?"

Di couldn't speak. She could barely breathe. She held her head in her hands, realizing she hadn't thought of Kari's reaction to finding her body.

"It doesn't matter," Di finally replied, and her voice broke. "Dad is going to kill me."

"No, Di. He's not going to touch you. Brantley and I are going to take care of you now. I'm sorry I didn't tell you before, but I was afraid you would talk about it. You're a terrible liar."

"What . . .?"

"I told you, I have a plan."

"Right." Di sniffed. Her neck was starting to ache, as the shock wore off. "You're never going to find a job in California. There's nothing in this stupid town. You're going to have to move, and I'll be alone with Dad."

"No. I have a *really good* plan."

"Tell me, then."

"Will that keep you from swan-diving off the roof?"

Di shrugged.

Kari put her hands on Di's shoulders. " , , , Home insurance isn't the only kind of insurance we could live on."

Di frowned.

"Dad has life insurance from his work. So if he dies . . . we get the money."

"So . . .?"

"We'll just say he ignored the burn unit doctors and took way too many pain pills — and then drank. It could kill a horse, what he downed tonight."

"You mean you gave him pills?"

"I crushed them into his drinks. The cocktail will kill him 'accidentally,' so we'll be worry free and rich before long." She sighed. "This is why I needed to get you out of that house. I was so afraid Dad would scare you or you would try to hurt yourself . . . Just go sleep in Officer Brantley's house. I'll take you."

Di followed Kari out of the bathroom. As they passed through the small living area, she threw all of her weight on top of her father and pounded on his chest.

"Dad! Wake up!"

But Kari pinned her arms to her sides and Di struggled to find her feet, until Kari lifted her over the shoulder and covered her mouth. A minute later, after Kari had crossed the backyard and knocked, Officer Brantley let them through the backdoor of his house.

"She's just upset," Kari grunted to him. "We'll be fine. Thanks for letting us in."

The officer nodded and left, as if Kari wasn't assaulting Di before his eyes.

"If you promise not to scream, I won't tape you up," Kari told Di, once he'd gone.

Di nodded.

Kari removed her hand. "Don't worry. He's out and he won't feel a thing. Now I'm going to go to sleep, and you're going to stay here and sleep. Got it?"

Di nodded again, eyes downcast.

Kari left, muttering to herself. "Dammit, where's my phone?"

Di waited until they disappeared into the smoke. Then she pulled Kari's phone out of her sweatshirt pocket, where she'd stashed it during the tussle. She stared at it, thinking of the words of Detective Bounds: "Don't do it. It'll get you sent to a juvenile hall somewhere out of county. It's a pain."

She dialed 911.

She had to be quick. Kari usually outsmarted her.

When the operator answered, she said, "My name is Diana Coburn and I need to report an arson. Two arsons. I . . . set them both. One is getting out of control right now and my sister is trying to put it out."

After giving the address, she hung up the phone even though dispatch was still asking questions. She closed her eyes and retreated to her abbey.

Officer Brantley arrested her a few hours later.

GENDER AND THE IMAGO DEI: TOGETHER WE REFLECT THE IMAGE OF GOD

Annie Crawford on Marriage's Divine Purpose

In his Ransom Trilogy, C.S. Lewis ironically harnesses the futuristic genre of science fiction to retrieve something very old: what it means to be human. Lewis had warned, in his 1943 lecture series *The Abolition of Man,* that if the old view is correct and man is fundamentally an incarnated being with a given form and purpose, then any reduction of "our own species to the level of mere Nature" will ruin us.[1] Throughout the Ransom Trilogy, Lewis's fictional counterpart to *The Abolition of Man,* Lewis challenges modern materialism by depicting space not as a cold, dead vacuity but as an "empyrean ocean of radiance," full of spiritual, transcendent

---

[1] C.S. Lewis, *The Abolition of Man* (New York: HarperCollins, 2001), 71.

life.[2] This setting in the heavenly "field of Arbol" opens up imaginative space for a renewed understanding of the cosmos and human nature.[3] Lewis asks us to imagine, what if modern materialists are wrong? What if our universe is crammed with meaning and every planet afire with the glory of God? And what if scientific inquiry is the very thing that leads us to re-discover an enchanted cosmos full of meaningful forms and divine purpose?

As the trilogy unfolds, Lewis surprises his readers by making his sci-fi space adventure into a story about gender. As the philologist hero, Ransom, rediscovers the spiritual life that fills the cosmos, he finds the dynamic between male and female ordering everything. Accordingly, the polarity of gender provides the narrative framework for the whole trilogy. In the first book, *Out of the Silent Planet*, Lewis sends Ransom to the masculine planet of Mars, which he calls Malacandra; in the second he travels to Venus, the feminine planet, which Lewis names Perelandra; and in the final installment, Ransom returns to Earth where Lewis portrays the

---

[2] C.S. Lewis, *Out of the Silent Planet* (New York: HarperCollins, 2001), 34.

[3] C.S. Lewis, *Perelandra* (New York: HarperCollins, 2001), 182.

reconciliation of genders through the restoration of the Studdocks' marriage. By wedding modern science fiction with baptized imagery of the mythological Mars and Venus, Lewis proposes a redeemed understanding of human nature through a cosmic vision of gender.

In other words, Lewis's ultimate answer to the problems of modernity is to affirm the Biblical doctrine of gender and marriage. How do we respond to the dehumanizing crisis of modernity? "Let marriage be held in honor among all, and let the marriage bed be undefiled."[4] Because the reality of gender originates in the relational nature of the Holy Trinity, which is reflected in the spiritual relationship between God and Man, Lewis knew that a sanctified understanding of masculine and feminine realities would be essential to the restoration of our full humanity. It is in the union of male and female together that we reflect the *imago Dei* and our essential human nature. When Genesis tells us that "God created mankind in his own image," the author takes care to emphasize that "in the image of God he created *them*."[5] Genesis 2 further develops this doctrine of the inherently

---

[4] Hebrews 13:4a, ESV.

[5] Gen. 1:27, emphasis mine.

relational *imago Dei* by showing us that it is "*not good for man to be alone.*"[6] The man alone does not reflect the nature of the intrinsically relational Godhead. God considers his *imago Dei* creation complete and "very good"[7] only when both male and female have been created and joined together.[8]

In the Genesis account, man was created first because the masculine gender analogically reflects the Father who is the creator of all things. The very words *man* and *woman* express this generative and temporal ordering — the word woman is formed from the root word man as the woman was taken out of the man, flesh of his flesh.[9] Reflecting this order, Lewis makes Mars/Malacandra older than Venus/Perelandra, as Adam was older than Eve. The Queen of Perelandra, Tenedril, echoes this ontology when she explains to Weston, "the King is always older than I, and about all things."[10] For the King to be the younger than the Queen would be "like a tree

---

[6] Gen. 2:18, emphasis mine.

[7] Gen. 1:31.

[8] Gen. 2:24.

[9] The English forms of *man* and *woman* parallel the Hebrew forms used in Genesis 2:22: man is אִישׁ or *ish* and woman, or the "out of man", is מֵאִישׁ or *meish*.

[10] Lewis, *Perelandra*, 90.

with no fruit" or "a fruit with no taste."[11] It is a logical impossibility. How can the Creator be younger than the created? Therefore, the man who symbolically embodies the initiating Creator must also come first and be created before the woman who embodies the beloved creation. We must not think reductionistically here — it is not that man is literally the creator of woman, but that the order of their genesis analogically reflects the relationship between God and creation.

This temporal ordering also reflects the atemporal hierarchy present in the Godhead itself. Although there has never been a time when the Father existed without the Son, still an ontological hierarchy exists within the Trinity. The Son is begotten of the Father and the Holy Spirit exists as the third, unifying resolution of this divine binary. In the polarity of gender, the masculine nature comes first, ordained by God to embody the originating Father. However, divine hierarchy does not logically entail an inequality of persons. Trinitarian theology establishes the equality of hierarchically-ordered genders. As the Son is begotten of the Father yet co-equal in eternal being and glory, so the feminine is created in response to

---

[11] Lewis, *Perelandra*, 90.

the masculine yet is also co-equal and co-existent with it. As the Godhead exists in an ordered yet co-equal unity of being, so the masculine and the feminine form an ordered yet co-equal unity.[12] And as in the Godhead, the Holy Spirit reconciles the binary of genders into a greater unity that is manifested both in the sacrament of marriage and in the union of Christ with His Bride.

Since man was created first, Ransom begins his mission to deliver earth from the destructive forces of modernity by traveling to the archaic, masculine world of Malacandra. To embody the masculine spirit of Mars/Malacandra, everything on the planet is shaped by a leitmotif of perpendicularity; the whole world is ordered vertically to express the firm, upright physiology of the male body. In *Planet Narnia,* Michael Ward observes that throughout the world of this Martial planet, "we encounter things that are described as high, narrow, steep, pointed, elongated, 'needling.' We find soaring columns,

---

[12] At the end of *That Hideous Strength,* Lewis makes a small allusion to the possibility of more than two genders. However, this is a moment where I believe Lewis let his imagination run away with him. Lewis's proposal here is a highly speculative idea that seems driven merely by his love of the Medieval cosmos and desire to retrofit theology into his imaginative cosmology. Further, if any such thing as extra-binary gender could exist, it would be irrelevant to the nature of human gender; we would, as Lewis says, "have no clue to them." C.S. Lewis, *That Hideous Strength* (New York: HarperCollins, 2001), 322.

pinnacle, pillars."[13] The mountains are a "riot of rock, leaping and surging skyward like solid jets from some rock-fountain,"[14] and the waves of water shoot up "far too high for their length, to narrow at the base, too steep in the sides."[15]

To understand Lewis, we must not perceive this imagery as "simply sexual."[16] Gender is not a projection of or an abstraction *from* biological sex; it is a transcendent, spiritual reality that is manifested in distinct ways within male and female creatures. Lewis explicitly states that the meaning of gender cannot be reduced to "an imaginative extension of sex."[17] Gender is "a more fundamental reality than sex. Sex is, in fact, merely the adaptation to organic life of a fundamental polarity which divides all created beings."[18] The word *gender* originates from the Greek root *gen* which means *birth* or *that which produces.* It is the root word for *genus, genesis, generate,* and *genital,* and it refers to the manner in

---

[13] Michael Ward, *Planet Narnia: The Seven Heavens in the Imagination of C.S. Lewis*, (Oxford: Oxford University Press, 2010), 81.

[14] Lewis, *Silent Planet*, 87.

[15] Ibid., 44.

[16] Ibid.

[17] Lewis, *Perelandra*, 171.

[18] Ibid., 172.

which life is produced or generated. The character of the masculine gender is rooted in the being of God who generates all other being and gives it form. All created being exists as the feminine reception of this divine generative action. Only a bent mind, as the Malacandrian *hrossa* would say, insists on reducing gendered imagery to mere sexual meanings; the Christian imagination perceives these material images as portals into deeper realities. The Christian cosmos is sacramental — meaning, the material realm is an embodied manifestation of the spiritual realm. The realities of this world teach us about the realities of heaven; trees teach us about righteousness, water about forgiveness, fire about judgment, and shepherding about God's care. Likewise, sex teaches us about a gendered polarity woven into the fabric of creation itself. Thus, the perpendicularity of the Malacandrian landscape should not engender a fixation on sex but rather a meditation on the self-giving virility and moral courage that is more truly at the center of the masculine identity.

As Ransom sojourns in Malacandra, he is transformed by the masculine spirit that presides over the entire planet. The Malacandrian people - the *hrossa, sorns*, and *pfifltriggi*, as well as the *eldils* and the *Oyarsa* - all live in stratified harmony under the righteous, generative rule of Maleldil, Lewis's fictional name for God. Because God the Creator is necessarily greater than His creatures, hierarchy is inherent to the fabric of the cosmos and a sense of duty is essential to masculine virtue.[19] As a Christian, Lewis also knows that Jesus Christ has shown the true masculine spirit to be characterized by deep love and self-sacrifice. Therefore, the masculine virtues of Malacandra are those which enable God's creatures to express His sacrificial love for the sake of others: obedience, moral integrity, courage, and fortitude. As Ransom learns from the *hrossa* and the Malacandrian ways, the martial spirit of the planet begins "to work a change in him."[20] Ransom grows in the masculine characteristics of a virtuous knight committed to his King; his courage, resolve, vigilance, and rectitude are developed and tested. On his first day in Malacandra, Lewis describes Ransom as full of "whimpering, unanalyzed, self-nourishing, self-consuming

---

[19] While all creatures — both men and women — have duties, the firm and unwavering nature of obedience is more clearly manifested in the straightness and rigidity of the male form. Men and women both possess all the masculine and feminine virtues — women are to be courageous and men are to be nurturing — but in different proportions and capacities. Men will never suckle a baby and as Lewis puts it, war is ugly when women fight.

[20] Lewis, *Silent Planet*, 79.

dismay."[21] But after Hyoi's death, Ransom finally learns to fully submit to the cosmic hierarchy which reigns over Malacandra. In his proper obedience to the Oyarsa, "in the clear light of accepted duty, he felt fear indeed, but with it a sober sense of confidence in himself and in the world, and even an element of pleasure."[22] Ransom has become courageous and resolute, prepared in his "new-found manhood" to complete hard duties for the sake of others and face death directly rather than compromise his moral integrity.[23]

Now a sanctified vessel of holy masculinity, Ransom journeys to the womb-like paradise of Perelandra, the feminine planet. Unlike the cold, archaic, and vertical landscape of Malacandra, Perelandra is warm and young and verdant. Through this sensuous vision of Venus, Lewis dares to celebrate something the modern imagination detests: the beauty of feminine submission. Because the masculine gender reflects the generative activity of the Creator God and the feminine gender reflects the receptivity of created being, masculine virtue is expressed as obedient action and feminine virtue is

---

[21] Lewis, *Silent Planet*, 87.

[22] Ibid., 87.

[23] Ibid., 81.

expressed as trusting responsiveness. This is why in ancient mythologies, the heavens are seen as masculine (Chronos) and the earth is seen as femenine (Gaia). Matter is essentially feminine in character because it receives the form which the Father gives it. Thus, receptivity is at the very center of cosmic femininity; it is the means by which new life and relationship are created.

While Ransom's climactic battle with the Un-man proves a distinctly masculine duty, to enter Perelandra, he must first align himself with her receptive character. Although he does not understand everything it means or how it will be accomplished, Ransom responds to the *eldil's* call to come to Perelandra with the trusting spirit of Mary; "Behold, I am the servant of the Lord; let it be to me according to your word."[24] As he sojourns in Perelandra, Ransom grows in this feminine posture of Marian receptivity. Whenever he is tempted to assert his independence or resist Maleldil's presence, "the very air seem[s] too crowded to breathe."[25] Ransom learns that "when you gave in to the thing, gave yourself up to it," the submission itself became "a medium, a sort of splendor as of eatable,

[24] Luke 1:38.

[25] Lewis, *Perelandra*, 62.

drinkable, breathable gold, which fed and carried you and not only poured into you but out from you as well."[26]

Yet this place of feminine submission is not oppressive; it is paradise. Everything in Perelandra is soft, fluid, scented, and curved — saturated with jewel-toned color and sensuous pleasure. Ransom's experience on Perelandra is full of pleasures. While he is still bobbing about the ocean after just arriving, he drinks the water. "It was almost like meeting Pleasure itself for the first time. He buried his flushed face in the green translucence."[27] The yellow balloon fruit of the Perelandran trees gave Ransom a sensation which seemed like a "totally new genus of pleasure."[28] By weaving together the sensuous imagery of Venus with the holy spirit of the Virgin Mary, Lewis challenges our debased inclination to imagine the submissive character of femininity as a prim prudery or misogynist construct. Wherever the masculine presence is one of rightly ordered, self-sacrificing love, the vulnerability of feminine submission brings intimate communion and deepest joy.

---

[26] Lewis, *Perelandra*, 62.

[27] Ibid. 32.

[28] Ibid., 37.

Through Ransom's victory over the Un-man, Lewis develops a distinctly Christological meaning to the union of masculine and feminine realities. On the cross, Christ our warrior poured out His life for the sake of His Bride; He defeated the darkness that had condemned her to death, and in this victory, He seeded the birth of a new redeemed humanity. He made the one flesh union of Adam and Eve an image not only of life-generating, Trinitarian communion, but also of redemption. Marriage has become the embodied promise of the union between Christ and His Church.[29] Ransom's battle with the invading evil partakes in Christ's redemptive and generative sacrifice. Ransom's self-sacrificial battle with Weston is an imitation of Calvary. As he struggles on the island garden of Perelandra to submit his will to the terror of his task, Ransom endures his own Gethsemane. When Ransom attacks the Un-man, the demon controlling Weston's body predicts that Ransom will suffer as one "nailed on to crosses."[30] Following the pattern of Christ's descent into Hell, Ransom nearly drowns as the demon pulls him down into the dark, cavernous bowels of Perelandra. And like the triumphant sacrifice of Christ,

---

[29] Eph. 5:31-32.

[30] Lewis, *Perelandra*, 130.

Ransom's metaphorical death for the sake of Perelandra sows the seed of new life for her people.

The consummation of Ransom's masculine self-sacrifice and Perelandra's feminine reception is achieved in a scene of sacred bliss. After defeating the Un-Man, Ransom ascends from the underworld of Perelandra until he reaches the most high and holy place on the planet. Ransom lies on sweet-scented slopes and climbs through parting mists; he comes before a pass between two rose-red peaks where he catches a glimpse of something soft and flushed, a garden "clothed in flowers."[31] He has come to Venus and offered himself up utterly to her, pouring out his life for her redemption. He is the embodiment of the true Bridegroom come in self-sacrificing love for His Bride. He is worthy "to enter that secret place," and this redemptive union generates new life.[32] As Mary was overshadowed by the Holy Spirit to bring forth the New Adam, so a bright, supernatural light overshadows this sacred garden where Ransom receives the reunited Tor and Tinidril. At this sacred moment, the ransomed King and Queen rise over the edge of this holy mountain, a radiant image of Christ and His Bride, so full of

---

[31] Lewis, *Perelandra*, 165

[32] Ibid.

beauty and glory and such a "masterpiece of self-portraiture"[33] that Ransom falls at their feet and confesses, "I have never before seen a man or a woman. I have lived all my life among shadows." [34] Through this wedding of Martial courage, self-sacrifice, vigilance, and rectitude with Venereal sweetness, pleasure, submission, and beauty, Lewis offers his readers a holy and glorious vision of God's sacramental design for the nuptial embrace.

In the final book of the Ransom Trilogy, *That Hideous Strength,* Lewis returns his story to Earth where gendered realities and the sacrament of marriage are distorted and decaying. After illuminating the transcendent, ideal reality of gender through his baptized vision of Mars and Venus, Lewis lastly reveals how the disorder on Earth can be healed through the restoration of marriage. The word "Matrimony" begins this final book of the trilogy and the renewed marital embrace of Jane and Mark concludes it. While appearing to be a dystopian adventure examining the dangers of scientism — something moderns like — Lewis is really writing a defense of traditional marriage — something moderns struggle to like. Lewis is here at

---

[33] Lewis, *Perelandra,* 177.

[34] Ibid., 176.

work, as in all his fiction, seeking to sneak sacred truths past the watchful dragons of modern resistance.

Alone in her kitchen, Jane Studdock bitterly recites a few words from the Anglican marriage ceremony: "Matrimony was ordained, thirdly … for the mutual society, help, and comfort."[35] At the beginning of *That Hideous Strength*, the Studdock marriage is not one of intimacy and comfort. The couple sees little of each other, and when they are together, there is little communion between them. Mark is preoccupied with his career and desires only "to cut a good figure in the eyes of his wife" as he seeks to feed his own ego while Jane is resentful of his self-centered claims on her affection and resists being vulnerable in any way.[36]

Mark later realizes that their modern, objectified approach to all reality had made them look on marriage as a contractual, self-centered arrangement. Their "laboratory outlook upon love, . . . had forestalled in Jane the humility of a wife [and] equally forestalled in him . . . the humility of a lover."[37] Jane wished to love Mark not as a

---

[35] Lewis, *Hideous Strength*, 11.

[36] Ibid., 87.

[37] Ibid., 378.

responsive, vulnerable counterpart but as an independent person, a spousal colleague of sorts. She resents her prophetic dreams because they intrude on "the bright, narrow little life which she had proposed to live."[38] Moderns see nature not as something with an inherent meaning or purpose which we must honor and obey, but as raw material onto which we can impose our will. Likewise, Mark and Jane saw their relationship as raw material they could arrange and bend to suit their selfish will. Mark does not want to see in his marriage some sacred order to which his career must bend; likewise, Jane does not "want to get drawn in" to either true union with Mark or with the numinous and unknown will of God.[39] She wants "something civilized, or modern . . . which did not want to possess her . . . something without hands that gripped and without demands upon her."[40] As the Director tells her later, she is "offended by the masculine itself, the gold lion, the bearded bull – which breaks through hedges and scatters the little kingdom of your primness."[41] Jane is offended by

---

[38] Lewis, *Hideous Strength*, 81.

[39] Ibid.

[40] Ibid., 313.

[41] Ibid., 312-313.

God — analogically reflected in the masculine — who would dare give her life a sacred form she must receive and obey. Moderns exist to make themselves, not to submit to what God has made them.

Perhaps we can forgive Jane for her resistance to the Divine Bridegroom, for her husband, Mark, is an insipid male who is unaware of his wife's inner conflicts and emotionally absent from the marriage. He is one of Lewis's "Men without Chests," a "mere trousered ape," whose modern education has atrophied his moral imagination and manly rectitude.[42][43] His mind is full of abstractions and his body full of unsanctified desires. The "things that he read and wrote [were] more real to him than things he saw. Statistics about agricultural labourers were the substance; any real ditcher, ploughman, or farmer's boy, was the shadow."[44] Mark's life has become, not a masculine imitation of Maleldil, but a compulsive effort to satisfy his own egocentric needs.

Yet the Studdock marriage begins to heal as both Mark and Jane learn submission to the love of Maleldil. Jane begins to change first after she visits

---

[42] Lewis, *Abolition*, 25.

[43] Ibid., 9.

[44] Lewis, *Hideous Strength*, 85.

St. Anne's and is stunned by the Director's presence. "For the first time in all those years she tasted the word *King* itself with all linked associations of battle, marriage, priesthood, mercy, and power."[45] As she experiences sanctified, self-sacrificing masculinity through Ransom, Jane begins to accept the receptive, responsive nature of femininity. She discovers that her prim and independent world is an impossibility, that "what is above and beyond all things is so masculine that we are all feminine in relation to it."[46] The "gold lion" is the very presence of God in relation to His creatures. The world is saturated with the masculine presence of God; there is no neutral ground on which to stand safely apart from this cosmic dance. Jane realizes that we must first give ourselves to the love of God before we can then give ourselves in love to others. It is through the obedient ordering of all things beneath the good and perfect will of God that we can then have joyful communion with Him and all He has created. She and Mark had "lost love because [they] never attempted obedience" to God.[47] Alone in the quiet

---

[45] Lewis, *Hideous Strength*, 140.

[46] Ibid., 313.

[47] Ibid., 145.

garden, Jane's defenses are laid aside and she becomes His.

More slowly, in the hellish halls of the N.I.C.E., Mark Studdock also begins to learn obedience to God. When his Jane's life is clearly threatened, he begins to wake from his eunuched stupor; the latent masculinity of this martial son is finally awakened by godly love for his wife. Swearing that "nothing but physical impossibility would stop him from going to Edgestow and warning Jane,"[48] Mark finally demonstrates masculine rectitude and courageous resolve. When faced with death, Mark awakes to see the world as it really is, not as a confusion of objects and circumstances to manipulate for the inflation of his own ego, but as a cosmos full of wonders and realities never dreamed of in his reductionist philosophy. He realizes how his perverse objectification of Jane had turned him into "the coarse, male boor . . . blundering, sauntering, stumping in where great lovers, knights and poets would have feared to tread."[49] Mark has discovered his own creaturely, feminine submission to God, and in this humble obedience to the King, he is now

---

[48] Lewis, *Hideous Strength*, 210.

[49] Ibid., 379.

ready to be a vessel of masculine, self-giving love to Jane.

After Mark and Jane are sanctified in their gendered roles, Venus descends on St. Anne's to consummate their reconciliation. She has come "to make Earth sane."[50] The brokenness of the Studdocks' modern marriage is healed by a restored acceptance of gender and what it teaches them about the right ordering of reality. Their feminine submission to God's creative initiative restores them to right relationship with God and each other. The air grows sweet and warm, and the couples begin to pair off as the animals gather to join the free, gendered dance in all its joy and romp. For one night on Earth, all is well ordered beneath the deeply good will of Maleldil. The masculine and the feminine are not in their self-consumed and distrusting, vulgar and resentful war with one another. All is humility and self-offering and obedience before the created order. In this unshadowed communion of sweet, overflowing life, in the warm union of open souls, there is holy ecstasy.

---

[50] Lewis, *Hideous Strength*, 376.

As Ransom explained to Jane, "obedience – humility – is an erotic necessity."[51] All men and women are made in the image of God and therefore equally good and valuable, yet, if we insist upon equality as the deepest reality in our relationships, the greatest thing we have, then the great dance simply ceases. In this frozen truce, where the commerce between souls must be equally calculated and economically measured, there is no joy, no gift of self, no charity. It is no union at all. Eros is our longing to be joined with something higher than ourselves. So the Apostle Paul tells us that to "be devoted to one another in love" you must "honor one another above yourselves." The deepest cosmic reality is not a static equality but the "Great Dance" of eros and charity that originates in the overflowing, generative love of the Triune God.[52]

If we have received Lewis's vision of gendered union aright, we, like Merlin, will feel "the inconsolable wound with which man is born."[53] The human soul was made for ecstasy, *to be taken out of oneself* into a higher reality. Yet like Jane, we moderns are especially "offended by the masculine

---

[51] Lewis, *Hideous Strength*, 146.

[52] Lewis, *Perelandra*, 183.

[53] Lewis, *Hideous Strength*, 320.

itself: . . . the gold lion, the bearded bull – which breaks through hedges and scatters the little kingdom of [our] primness."[54] We do not want to walk in the feminine humility of creatures, so in our rebellion against God we deconstruct, deny, and distort the gendered reality of the cosmos. Rather than honor women rightly, through interventions like contraceptives, abortion, and daycare we try to liberate them from all that is actually feminine. The brokenness of the modern world can only be healed by a restored acceptance of gender and what it teaches us about right ordering of reality.

It will be by our feminine submission to God's creative, redeeming initiative that we are restored to right relationship with God and one another. We resist the transcendent reality of gender, but our very bodies stubbornly testify against us. Our gendered bodies are telling us the Gospel; Christ our Bridegroom has offered Himself to us if we will only receive him with humility in return. It will be by our feminine submission to God's creative, redeeming initiative that we are restored to right relationship with God and one another.

---

[54] Lewis, *Hideous Strength*, 312-313.

A Silent Genocide:
Disability and the
Ongoing Consequences of
Social Darwinism

Zak Schmoll on the Tragedy of Eugenics

Disability is a term that is difficult to define, but much like G.K. Chesterton said of the term eugenics, "I know that it means very different things to different people; but that is only because evil always takes advantage of ambiguity."[1] The eugenics movement utilized any ambiguity in its own name to systematically, and legally, seek the genocidal elimination of people with disabilities. It did this by creating doubt about the fundamental humanity of people with disabilities, adding a layer of ambiguity where there should never have been one.

However, lest we feel like the human race has made sufficient moral progress to never even consider the organized eradication of members of

---

[1] G.K. Chesterton, *Eugenics and Other Evils* (New York: Cassell and Company, 1922), 3, Digital Edition.

our human family, these issues are more relevant than ever in our era of increased scientific knowledge and genetic testing. Down syndrome has been the most widely publicized example of a disability that, when diagnosed prenatally, leads to extraordinarily high abortion rates, almost universally attacking people on the basis of their genetic code.[2] Proponents argue that a mercy killing is necessary to prevent a life of suffering, but they are disregarding an important reality about human nature; all are made in the image of God, and God became one with us in our humanity.

The assault on the uniqueness of human creation began to gain momentum with the advent of Darwinism. With the Enlightenment-committed intelligentsia concluding that God was no longer necessary for creation, the concept that any were made in the image of God was suddenly no longer required. Humanity was just another type of animal with nothing differentiating it from other primates except for a few fortunate genetic developments.

If humans have no more value than any other part of the natural world, then maybe human

---

[2] Sarah Zhang, "The Last Children of Down Syndrome," *The Atlantic*, November 18, 2020, accessed December 29, 2020, https://www.theatlantic.com/magazine/archive/2020/12/the-last-children-of-down-syndrome/616928/.

institutions should be evaluated by Darwinian principles as well. Darwinism was accepted by Enlightenment scientists who wanted to understand the natural world without the supernatural, so perhaps it had explanatory power for social scientists with similar philosophical commitments as well. Enter Social Darwinism,

> a loose set of ideologies that emerged in the late 1800s in which Charles Darwin's theory of evolution by natural selection was used to justify certain political, social, or economic views. Social Darwinists believe in 'survival of the fittest'—the idea that certain people become powerful in society because they are innately better.[3]

Blending scientific theory with Nietzsche's will to power led to the idolatry of power and left an important question for these theorists. What do we do with those who are not powerful? What do we do with those who actually might need extra support to fully function in society?

Tragically, the answer to that question is most obviously illustrated in Nazi Germany which

---

[3] "Social Darwinism," *History*, last modified August 21, 2018, accessed December 29, 2020, https://www.history.com/topics/early-20th-century-us/social-darwinism.

termed such individuals "useless eaters."[4] What many people sometimes forget is that Hitler's first murderous step was to apply Darwinian principles to the human race. Those who were unable to survive independently did not deserve to live. Before he massacred millions upon millions of people for a variety of reasons, he tested his killing machine on individuals with disabilities. From 1939 until 1941, 70,000 people in Germany and Austria were euthanized, labeled as "unworthy of life."[5] Once the intrinsic value of each person was stripped away and the ability to survive and be of use to the state were the only metrics of value, hundreds, thousands, and ultimately millions were massacred utilizing a very similar justification.

Hitler is oftentimes cited as the exemplar of evil, and for good reason. One could contend that because he was an extraordinarily evil individual at the head of a powerful political machine, such terrible things

---

[4] Mark P. Mostert, "Useless Eaters: Disability as Genocidal Marker in Nazi Germany," *Catholic Culture*, 2002, accessed December 29, 2020, https://www.catholicculture.org/culture/library/view.cfm?recnum=7019.

[5] "The Murder of People with Disabilities | The Holocaust Encyclopedia," *United States Holocaust Memorial Museum*, accessed December 29, 2020, https://encyclopedia.ushmm.org/content/en/article/the-murder-of-the-handicapped.

would not happen among most ordinary people. Eugenics is so obviously evil, you might think it was only practiced by those extraordinarily terrible people like Hitler. Sadly, the history of eugenics extends to our own country as well, and my own alma mater on a personal note. I completed my undergraduate studies at the University of Vermont. Dr. Henry F. Perkins, a professor of zoology, conducted the Eugenics Survey of Vermont beginning in 1925. This study, which directly influenced policy decisions, led to the sterilization of over 200 women who were labeled "mentally deficient."[6] Perkins also wanted to have a "Better Family Contest" at Vermont state fairs to promote eugenics in small towns, showing all the good they were doing by creating better genealogical specimens.[7] The sterilization numbers are far from those in Nazi Germany, but Perkins's evil impulses stemmed from the same root and manifested themselves in several of the same ideas that

---

[6] "Vermont Eugenics," *Eugenics: Compulsory Sterilization in 50 American States*, accessed December 29, 2020, http://www.uvm.edu/~lkaelber/eugenics/VT/VT.html.

[7] "Letter, H.F. Perkins to W.C. Palmer, American Eugenics Society,. May 27, 1930," *Vermont Eugenics: A Documentary History*, accessed December 29, 2020, http://www.uvm.edu/~eugenics/primarydocs/olhpaes052730.xml.

enamored the Nazis, even if they were not put into practice to such a devastating degree.

Perkins was so influential that Margaret Sanger, the founder of what eventually became Planned Parenthood, wrote to him asking for his support for her birth control legislation. She called Perkins one of many "outstanding authorities" who she was hoping to get to support her legislation.[8] He responded to her with great enthusiasm, saying,

From the point of view of humanitarian attitude, there is reason to promulgate birth control. Economically it would reduce the number of unemployed, paupers and those dependent on society because of mental and physical defects. None of these reasons to my mind is nearly so important from the broad point of view as the eugenical reason--the importance of breeding a higher type of people.[9]

---

[8] "Letter, Margaret Sanger to Henry F. Perkins, . February 9, 1933," *Vermont Eugenics: A Documentary History*, accessed December 29, 2020, http://www.uvm.edu/~eugenics/primarydocs/olmshfp020933.xml

[9] "Letter, H.F. Perkins to Margaret Sanger, . February 11, 1933," *Vermont Eugenics: A Documentary History*, accessed December 29, 2020, http://www.uvm.edu/~eugenics/primarydocs/olhfpms021133.xml .

Sanger herself was such a proponent of eugenics that even Planned Parenthood of New York recently disavowed her over her views.[10]

Despite the distance that Planned Parenthood of New York attempted to put between themselves and their eugenicist founder, abortion itself, as referenced above in the example regarding Down syndrome, provides the means of selectively breeding today. Even extraordinarily pro-abortion publications like *Slate* acknowledge,

> In many parts of Europe, including the United Kingdom, the termination rate after a prenatal Down syndrome diagnosis is now more than 90 percent. In Iceland, where testing is widespread, "we have basically eradicated, almost, Down syndrome from our society," one geneticist told CBS last year. In Denmark, where all pregnant women have been offered screening scans since 2004, the disorder is heading for "extinction."[11]

---

[10] Nikita Stewart, "Planned Parenthood in N.Y. Disavows Margaret Sanger Over Eugenics," *The New York Times*, July 21, 2020, accessed December 29, 2020, https://www.nytimes.com/2020/07/21/nyregion/planned-parenthood-margaret-sanger-eugenics.html.

[11] Ruth Graham, "Choosing Life With Down Syndrome," *Slate*, May 31, 2018, accessed December 29, 2020, https://slate.com/human-interest/2018/05/how-down-syndrome-is-redefining-the-abortion-debate.html.

To say that abortion does not allow those similar Social Darwinist, eugenicist impulses to live on in our society today is simply disingenuous.

This progression of Social Darwinist thought has developed over the past century and a half to create a culture where, even if many will not admit it, human value is anchored in survival value and perceived usefulness. We have rejected the reality that man was specially created in the image of God and have replaced it with a societal construct of value that elevates these utilitarian elements to its chief virtue.

It is one of the many jobs of the Christian, then, to reject these dehumanizing tendencies and restore a holistic and robust definition of human value, especially for those who society has oftentimes sought to diminish. How should we do this?

Perhaps the first myth to dispel is that individuals with disabilities are subhuman in any way. This is the myth that eugenicists consistently promote. Logically, their argument is severely lacking. All of humanity exhibits a variety of ability and disability. Some people are more intelligent, and some people are less intelligent; some people are physically stronger, and some people are physically weaker. Ability and disability are continuums, so to choose an arbitrary cutoff point based on one measure of ability or disability does not make logical sense when determining value. Human value is not a measure like an exam score where it is easy to determine that someone answered sixty percent of the multiple-choice questions correctly. Rather, human ability is multidimensional. It is simply illogical to conclude that because of a low IQ or legs that cannot stand that someone has less value than someone else. Individuals with disabilities, therefore, seem to be just like everyone else — humans who exist with abilities of varying levels on a variety of scales that interact with each other in a complex, multidimensional way that cannot be reduced to one arbitrary measure of "worthiness to live."

If individuals with disabilities are just as human as anyone else without a disability, then the next question to consider is why humankind in general has value. After all, Social Darwinism has historically led to the extermination of those deemed "unfit" and led to the promotion of those who are "fittest." However, fitness of survival is a very poor measure of value. As a somewhat parallel example, gold has a great deal of value, but its value is not determined by its ability to survive. Rather, its value is determined by the price that someone will pay for it. When more people want to buy it, the price goes up, but gold has not become any more fit to survive through that process. Albeit this is just one example, but it is quite clear that value is not always determined by fitness to survive. Even in a purely secular example, we intuitively seem to understand that there are other ways to define value.

Considering value as the price that someone is willing to pay, however, finds its ultimate fulfillment in the person of Jesus Christ. He came to earth to die for each and every one of us. That is how much He values each individual person; He gave His life for all humans, with disabilities and without. When asking questions of why the human race has value, it is quite clear that we are incredibly valuable to the Creator of the universe.

But the illustration extends even further because the sacrifice of Jesus Christ was not based on anything that we have done. Our value to God is not determined by what we can do for Him; "But God demonstrates His own love toward us, in that while we were still sinners, Christ died for us."[12] Our value was high enough simply because of who we are, humans created in the image of God, that He loved us and died for us.

---

[12] Romans 5:8, NKJV.

The Gospel is indeed the corrective to society's warped definition of human value that has led to so many atrocities, especially against people with disabilities. While the world creates arbitrary measures of value based on utilitarian metrics, God reaffirms that, "For God so loved the world that He gave His only begotten Son, that whoever believes in Him should not perish but have everlasting life."[13] All have sinned, and all have the ability to approach the throne of God and have everlasting life through Him. We have destroyed far too many lives by our radical acceptance of the destructive ideology of Social Darwinism, and apologists must show a superior way.

---

[13] John 3:16, NKJV.

Do You Long for Having Your Heart Interlinked?: The Imago Dei and Our Need for Relationships in the Blade Runner Universe

Megan Joy Rials on Love, Authenticity, and Reality

Blade Runner (BR) and *Blade Runner 2049* (*BR2049*) portray dystopian societies that both challenge Christian morals and pose questions to the Christian about essential aspects of humanity. The films present "replicants" that raise the issue of what it truly means to be human and made in the *imago Dei*. Whereas *BR* raises the issue of death as it relates to our humanity, *BR2049*, through its emphasis on birth and issues surrounding female reproduction, studies a crucial part of the *imago Dei*: our desire for community. Despite the bleakness the films present in their constant questioning of reality and the breakdown of community they portray, they serve as a reminder of God's creation and plan for us and show us a glimmer of hope in forging relationships with one another once again.

More Human than Human

The plots of both films revolve around "replicants," which the opening scene of the second film describes as "bioengineered humans."[1] The main character of *BR*, Rick Deckard, refers to them as "machines," but this characterization is misleading.[2] The replicants, called "more human than human," are created primarily to serve humans in various capacities.[3] *BR* features three different replicant models: combat, pleasure, and military. They are meant to duplicate humans but with superior physical resistance and speed and without emotions. The development of their emotions, however, eventually becomes the catalyst for the events of both films, particularly *BR*. Here, we will focus first on the importance of the body.

As Christians, we believe that to be made in the *imago Dei* entails two parts: the immaterial (the

---

[1] *Blade Runner 2049*, directed by Denis Villeneuve (Alcon Entertainment, Columbia Pictures, 2017), DVD (Warner Bros. Pictures, 2018).*Blade Runner*, directed by Ridley Scott. The Ladd Company, Shaw Brothers, 1982. DVD, Warner Home Video, 2007.

[2] *Blade Runner*, directed by Ridley Scott (The Ladd Company, Shaw Brothers, 1982), DVD (Warner Home Video, 2007).

[3] Ibid.

M. Rials   *The Imago Dei and Blade Runner*

mind and soul) and the material (the body).[4] The essential nature of the body is questioned in *BR2049*, where hologram personalities such as Joi, the girlfriend of the replicant main character, K, exist. Joi's awareness of others' preferences and mental states, such as the scene where she cycles through a variety of different outfits before settling on one K likes, indicates she is close to being able to reason about her own mental states.[5] Over the course of the film, Joi becomes a strong agent when she transcends her programming to satisfy the desires of her owner by instead recognizing her own conflicting desires and committing wholeheartedly to a decision or a desire. This point comes when she demands that K fully download her onto a device called an emanator, which renders her susceptible to the death of permanent destruction — "Like a real girl," as she puts it.[6] [7] There is a distinction to be made, however, between being a human being with its full attendant biological realities and having

---

[4] H.O. Mounce, "On Dualism," *New Blackfriars* 91, No. 1034 (July 2010): 406-407.

[5] Robert W. Clowes, "Breaking the Code: Strong Agency and Becoming a Person," in *Blade Runner 2049: A Philosophical Exploration*, eds. Timothy Shanahan and Paul Smart (New York: Routledge, 2020), 118-19.

[6] Ibid., 122-23.

[7] *Blade Runner 2049*, directed by Denis Villeneuve.

157

"personhood" by possessing many of our cognitive abilities, but not a body.[8] Under the Christian conception, Joi cannot possess the *imago Dei* because of her lack of a body.

The replicants, on the other hand, clearly possess the material part of the *imago Dei*. Further, they even possess DNA, as we discover when K and Joi visit an archive and comb through records of replicant DNA. Although we are not given details, the replicants' creation appears to take place in a lab and is artificial. Other than not gestating in a womb, however, they do not appear to possess any morally significant bodily differences from humans. The development of the replicants' emotions in *BR* raises the question: when replicants can be created who look and behave like humans, what are the distinguishing characteristics of the soul that signal its presence?

First, we will examine emotion. The question of whether replicants even possess emotions at all is central in *BR*. Deckard's boss indicates that replicants were "designed to copy human beings in every way, except their emotions. The designers reckoned that after a few years, they might develop their own emotional responses. You know, hate,

---

[8] Clowes, "Breaking the Code," 111.

love, fear, anger, envy."[9] Thus, it seems replicants were originally not supposed to have emotions but eventually developed them. Despite this, however, there is a suspicion that the replicants do not completely possess one key emotion: empathy. The film's fictional Voight-Kampf test, meant to distinguish replicants from humans, centers on a series of questions that expose a lack of empathy in the subject, such as whether the subject would help a tortoise being baked to death in the sun. The suggestion is that replicants would not help another in need.

In the course of the film, this assumption is challenged as Deckard, who is seemingly human, "retires" rogue replicants as part of his job as a blade runner — that is, he kills them.[10] The replicants, conversely, are concerned with their replicant friends' well-being and their short, four-year lifespans. Their leader, Roy Batty, is particularly insistent that their lifespan be extended. In another show of empathy, after a long chase scene following Deckard's retirement of Batty's replicant girlfriend, Pris, Batty has the opportunity to kill Deckard by

---

[9] *Blade Runner*, directed by Ridley Scott.

[10] The question of whether Deckard is a human or a replicant has been subject to much debate, but is not germane to this discussion.

dropping him off a building. Instead of taking revenge for Pris's death, however, he pulls Deckard up and spares his life.

Connected to this discussion of emotion is the replicants' ability for moral reasoning and their free will. In *BR2049*, K, a blade runner like Deckard, is tasked with "retiring" older models of replicants that are not as obedient as the Nexus-9, the replicant model of which K himself is a member. When his boss, Lieutenant Joshi, orders him to find and retire Deckard's child, who is at least half-replicant because the child's mother was a replicant, he replies, "I've never retired something that was born before."[11] She asks him why it matters, and K explains, "To be born is to have a soul, I guess."[12] Because of the inculcated idea that replicants are not human, K evidently does not consider the killing of other replicants to be immoral, but he seems to identify the killing of an entity with a soul as morally wrong. K continues to rebel against his orders to kill the replicant child and eventually reunites her with Deckard. This is K's moment of "wholeheartedness" when he proves himself a

---

[11] *Blade Runner 2049*, directed by Denis Villeneuve.

[12] Ibid.

strong agent.[13] Despite the assertion that the replicant model to which he belongs, Nexus-9, is obedient to human masters, K proves his free will by asserting his moral reasoning.

The replicants also possess both strong self-awareness and an awareness of death. In *BR*, one of the human characters, J. F. Sebastian, a genetic designer of the replicants, requests that Batty and Pris perform a trick for him. "We're not computers, Sebastian," Batty reminds him, and with a quote recalling Descartes, Pris chimes in, "I think, Sebastian, therefore I am."[14] In this exchange, we see the replicants' awareness of themselves and of their relation to the "lived body."[15] The replicants, led by Batty, have returned to Earth from their relative safety on other planets and risk their lives to find the owner of the Tyrell Corporation, the company that creates the replicants, to discover how they can outlive their preordained four-year lifespans.[16] Batty becomes incensed when Tyrell, the

---

[13] Clowes, "Breaking the Code," 124.

[14] *Blade Runner*, directed by Ridley Scott.

[15] Peter Atterton, "'More Human than Human': *Blade Runner* and Being-Toward-Death," in *Blade Runner*, eds. Amy Coplan and David Davies (New York: Routledge, 2015), 53-54.

[16] Because the replicants in *BR2049* have normal lifespans, this issue does not arise in the second film.

eponymous owner of the corporation, cannot extend their lifespan, hissing, "I want more life, father."[17] It is the dread of death that is "human *par excellence*" and separates humanity from animals, and it allows Batty, a replicant, to die an "authentic" death. Batty stands in contrast to the human Sebastian, who lives without an "essential anxiety" toward death and with a "banal everyday selfhood" that does not allow him to develop an "authentic self."[18]

The entire mood of the film, in fact, heightens the viewer's awareness toward death via the replicants' desperation to live longer. The lighting is consistently dark, and the gloomy *mise-en-scène* as a measure of character evokes the replicants' despair.[19] Many of the scenes are dreary with dirty city streets and constant rain. It is this grimness we recall as Tyrell assures Batty that although his life has been short, it has been spectacular: "The light that burns twice as bright burns half as long. And you have burned so very, very brightly, Roy. Look at

---

[17] *Blade Runner*, directed by Ridley Scott.

[18] Atterton, "More Human," 46-47, 54-55.

[19] Timothy Corrigan and Patricia White, *The Film Experience: An Introduction*, 3d ed., (Boston: Bedford/St. Martin's, 2004), 87.

you. You're the prodigal son. You're quite a prize!"[20] Batty reminds him, "I've done questionable things," which precedes his deadly reaction to Tyrell's flippant response to his worries and serves as a mirror to our feelings about ourselves.[21] Yes, we are all sinners who have done questionable things, but this knowledge does not lessen our desire to live; neither do reminders of our achievements comfort us when faced with the prospect of death.

Based on these factors — empathy, moral reasoning, free will, self-awareness, and an awareness of death — combined with the fact that the replicants are created from DNA in what is essentially an artificial birth process, the conclusion that the replicants possess souls and the *imago Dei* is inescapable. Most tellingly, when Batty dies, the dove he has been holding flies away, symbolizing his soul leaving his body.[22] One final element confirms that replicants possess the *imago Dei*: their desire for community. Batty is desperate for "more life" for his replicant friends and remains loyal to them even unto his death, and K searches for meaningful

---

[20] *Blade Runner*, directed by Ridley Scott.

[21] Ibid.

[22] Berys Gaut, "Elegy in LA: *Blade Runner*, Empathy and Death," in *Blade Runner*, eds. Amy Coplan and David Davies (New York: Routledge, 2015), 38.

relationships, whether with Joi or with his own family, when he believes he might have biological relatives. C.S. Lewis explains that because God is triune, He Himself is relational: "Love is something that one person has for another person. If God was a single person, then before the world was made, He was not love. . . . [I]n Christianity God is not a static thing — not even a person — but a dynamic, pulsating activity, a life, almost a kind of drama. Almost, if you will not think me irreverent, a kind of dance."[23] The replicants' desire for community is reflective of our need for relationships because we are made in the *imago Dei*. Just as God Himself is a personal, relational God, so we also desperately need community, as *BR2049* explores in great detail.

A Part of Us That's Missing

The human (and replicant) need for relationships is perhaps best seen in our society's epidemic of loneliness. The relational brokenness in our world manifests itself in a variety of ways: religious service attendance has declined; the average person in the United States says he has only one close friend; one in four people have no friends; more than two in ten adults in the United States and

---

[23] C.S. Lewis, *Mere Christianity* (New York: HarperOne, 1952), 174-75.

the United Kingdom say they always or often feel lonely; the average marriage age has risen; and fertility rates have declined.[24] Loneliness can be the culprit behind mental illnesses such as anxiety, depression, and schizophrenia, and it was recently discovered that it can be responsible for cellular inflammation that can lead to heart disease, stroke, metastatic cancer, and Alzheimer's disease.[25] Millennials identify loneliness as their primary fear, ahead of losing a home or a job, with 42% of women saying they fear loneliness more than a cancer diagnosis.[26] Because of the Covid-19 pandemic, this societal problem has intensified. Loneliness rates skyrocketed in 2020, with approximately 75% of men and women in the United States reporting that they feel lonelier because of the pandemic.[27] Clearly,

---

[24] Jillian Richardson, "Lonely? You're not alone. America's young people suffering from a lack of meaningful connection," *NBC News*, January 1, 2019, last accessed October 2, 2020, https://www.nbcnews.com/think/opinion/lonely-you-re-not-alone-america-s-young-people-are-ncna945446; Neil Howe, "Millennials and the Loneliness Epidemic," *Forbes*, May 3, 2019, last accessed October 2, 2020, https://www.forbes.com/sites/neilhowe/2019/05/03/millennials-and-the-loneliness-epidemic/#1c60ca6f7676.

[25] Richardson, "Lonely? You're not alone."

[26] Ibid.

[27] Jamie Ducharme, "COVID-19 is making America's loneliness epidemic worse," *TIME*, May 8, 2020, last accessed October 2, 2020, https://time.com/5833681/loneliness-covid-19/.

relationships with one another are necessary for us not only to thrive, but to survive. We see the effects of sin in the disruption and corruption of our relationships with our fellow man, which serve to deprive us of this essential aspect of life and the *imago Dei*.

BR2049 confronts our relational brokenness head-on and features the yearning for connection as one of its main themes. Many scenes throughout the film feature snow, whether floating down from above or compacted on the ground, both of which reflect the remoteness and iciness of the society portrayed.[28] The question of the humans' cold behavior is specifically raised in connection with the reproductive alterations in the design of female replicants and is intimately connected to the interpersonal brokenness portrayed in the film. As *BR* focused on death and the end of life, *BR2049* is conversely preoccupied with birth and the beginning of life. This interest reaches back to *BR*, in fact, where one of the questions in the Voight-Kampf test prompts the subject to discuss only good things that come to mind about his mother, and the replicant being tested shoots the administrator of the test to death. *BR2049* addresses issues

---

[28] Corrigan and White, *The Film Experience*, 87.

surrounding natality and its implications for relational problems in society.[29] The female replicants do not possess the ability to bear children, but after K discovers the remains of Rachael, Deckard's replicant girlfriend, and it is determined that she died after an emergency Caesarean section, the film reveals that she was an "experiment" capable of having children. Niander Wallace, head of the Wallace Corporation, which took over the production of replicants from the Tyrell Corporation, admits that the secret of creating female replicants who can bear children has eluded him.

The relational issues seen in the film are predominantly related to its society's twisted views of women and female replicants, which indicates that our tinkering with God's design for creation has disastrous effects on us and our relations with one another. There are two opposing misogynistic viewpoints in this society. The first is the idea that women should conform to the whims of men. This view is embodied in the very existence of the hologram Joi, which the Wallace Corporation sells to customers seeking companionship, promising that

---

[29] Brian Treanor, "Being-From-Birth: Natality and Narrative," in *Blade Runner 2049: A Philosophical Exploration*, eds. Timothy Shanahan and Paul Smart (New York: Routledge, 2020), 71-72.

she is "everything you want to hear."[30] This concept
of a woman customizable to every whim of the man
who owns her extends into the treatment of women
solely as sexual beings to please men. The Wallace
Corporation's advertisements in Los Angeles feature
a fully nude Joi beckoning to passersby. This
emphasis on the nude female form continues as K
tracks Deckard to Las Vegas and while traveling
through the desert encounters a series of statues of
nude women in suggestive poses.

The idea of women conforming to men's
preferences, especially the hypersexualized ideal
seen in the film's society, is destructive to the
formation of genuine relationships, whether
platonic or romantic, between men and women and
is particularly destructive to the institution of
marriage. Any woman, whether human or
hologram, who adapts her personality and actions
constantly to please a man is not behaving as a real
person, and such an expectation strips any human
relationship of its authenticity, both for the woman
whose personality is undermined by the charade
and the man for whose benefit she performs. This
kind of convenient "relationship" allows men to
have a shadow of the genuine article while dodging

---

[30] *Blade Runner 2049*, directed by Denis Villeneuve.

its inevitable challenges and responsibilities, particularly the marriage vow and the creation of a family. The film bears this out in that a mention of marriage is not even made, and no intact nuclear family unit is portrayed. This portrayal reflects our current society with its overall rise in divorce rates and the decline of the traditional, two-parent family.[31]

The second misogynistic view in *BR2049* is the marginalization of the female replicants for their lack of reproductive capabilities and finding their value only in their ability to produce children. Nowhere is this depicted more clearly than when Niander Wallace visits a newborn female replicant. She drops out of a sac and lies trembling before him and his female replicant assistant, Luv. After she gains enough strength to stand, Wallace ponders the mystery of natural reproduction and his anger over his failure to create female replicants with this ability. He observes, "Every leap of civilization was built off the back of a disposable workforce. We lost our stomach for slaves, unless engineered. But I can only make so many."[32] Concluding that she is

---

[31] "The American Family Today," *Pew Research Center*, December 17, 2015, https://www.pewsocialtrends.org/2015/12/17/1-the-american-family-today/.

[32] *Blade Runner 2049*, directed by Denis Villeneuve.

worthless, he murders the newborn replicant by slashing her abdomen with a scalpel where her womb would be. This view also results in the commoditization of children and, again, in the destruction of the nuclear family in its emphasis on children as products and slave labor.

Neither the first view nor the second view is Biblical because both reduce women to their worth strictly in relation to their bodies rather than properly focusing on women being made in the image of God and finding their value therein. As Dr. Holly Ordway has observed, "I came to realize that my identity as a woman is not dependent on marrying or having children ... I am a woman in all the fullness of my femininity because that is how God made me."[33] Under either of these views, women are not valued as complete individuals; they are appreciated only for the purposes their bodies can fulfill.

Two relationships in the film provide an interesting counterpoint and portrayal, respectively, of these two views. First, there is the relationship between K and Joi. Joi embraces her romance with K and appears consumed by it,

---

[33] Holly Ordway, "The Trauma of the Given," *Word on Fire*, January 5, 2018, https://www.wordonfire.org/resources/blog/the-trauma-of-the-given/5679/.

although her affection for K seems genuine and her desire for a "normal" relationship is noble in this unstable society. As discussed previously, Joi seems to have surpassed her programming to become a strong agent and to develop a real relationship with K. The question of the degree to which her love for K is merely the product of her programming is, however, a stumbling block to their relationship, because when Joi purrs, "I'm so happy when I'm with you," K immediately responds, "You don't have to say that."[34] K must help Joi transcend her programming, and based on his desire to help her do so, it seems he is also interested in a genuine relationship. It is noteworthy that given Joi's existence as a hologram, K's motivation for the relationship is not physical in nature. He apparently believes a relationship with a hologram is his best chance of creating a genuine bond, likely because as a replicant, he is treated as an outcast. K and Joi's relationship is the exception to this society's first view of women that proves the rule. He visits with Joi about his day after he returns home from work and purchases an emanator so that she can travel with him as his constant companion, which shows

---

[34] *Blade Runner 2049*, directed by Denis Villeneuve.

our innate desire for relationships — romantic or not — with others.

K and Joi's relationship is the only healthy one portrayed in the film, and significantly, K also struggles with the implications of possibly being the miracle replicant child of Rachael and Deckard before realizing he is not. In doing so, he must confront various relational issues, and thus it is not surprising Joi finds a good relationship with him. We see K pass his first baseline test, which has replaced the Voight-Kampf test to check for emotional stability — in reality, a lack of emotion — in replicants and asks such questions as "Do you long for having your heart interlinked?" and "Do you feel that there's a part of you that's missing?"[35] Later, though, he flunks his second baseline test, indicating that he has started to form relationships with others. The mere chance that he might be the replicant child serves as the catalyst for his desire to "explore his natality" by searching for his parents.[36] Issues surrounding natality necessarily involve social and relational issues because it reminds us of our embodied relationality with others and that we were born into a community that knew us before we

---

[35] *Blade Runner 2049*, directed by Denis Villeneuve.

[36] Treanor, "Being-From-Birth," 77.

knew them.[37] Even Joi, who does not possess the *imago Dei*, recognizes the inherent uniqueness of natural birth and the love inherent in the creation of life when she remarks to K, "I always knew you were special. Maybe this is how. A child. Of woman born. Pushed into the world. Wanted. Loved."[38] Our desire for community is similarly reflected in our desire for authentic relationships with others, because we are made in the *imago Dei* of the Triune, relational God — God the Father, God the Son, and God the Holy Spirit are in constant communion with one another, in a continual dance, as Lewis described it.[39] It should come as no surprise that the desire is inherent in us, and in replicants, as well.

The relationship between Luv and Niander Wallace, on the other hand, depicts the toxic, second misogynistic view and its damaging consequences. The ironically named Luv serves her master, Wallace, with a single-minded ferocity and has perhaps the greatest capacity for violence of any character in the film. In a scene of perverted femininity, she has her nails painted while she orders deadly drone strikes. Later, Luv casually

---

[37] Treanor, "Being-From-Birth," 71-72.

[38] *Blade Runner 2049*, directed by Denis Villeneuve.

[39] Lewis, *Mere Christianity*, 174-75.

murders Lieutenant Joshi in cold blood and attempts to kill K. Luv is aware her only inherent value to Wallace would lie in her capacity to reproduce: when he murders the newborn replicant, a tear slides down Luv's cheek, betraying her inner turmoil over his attitude toward female replicants. In a world where, under Wallace, she would be valued only for her reproductive capabilities, she instead embraces violence to win Wallace's approval. Denied the ability to create, Luv destroys, and destroys so effectively that she makes herself indispensable to Wallace. The bid succeeds, because even though she cannot reproduce, Wallace praises her as his "best angel."[40] Their relationship is warped beyond recognition of either friendship or romance because of Wallace's insistence on finding value in female replicants only in their childbearing capabilities. His distorted view of women results in Luv's desperate attempt to find another way to prove her worth to him and form at least a shadow of a connection with another being.

Thus, we see that the human alteration of female reproductive capacities has disastrous effects on civilization and on the characters' relationships with each other. It results in a society that overall

---

[40] *Blade Runner 2049*, directed by Denis Villeneuve.

does not appear to be that different from our own, with its distressing lack of genuine friendships, breakdown in local communities, high rate of promiscuity, decline of marriage, and destruction of the nuclear family unit as God designed it. In spite of the problems we create, however, our innate, God-given craving for connection with others continues to point us to the relational God we serve. As Lieutenant Joshi remarks to K, "We're all just looking for something real."[41] *BR2049* offers a glimmer of the "something real" God's plan contains for us in the connection K and Joi forge and in the hints of the only family mentioned in the film.

Looking for Something Real

Before going any further, we must ask the question: do humans act as good stewards of God's creation in their development and treatment of replicants? Based on the disruptive societal effects of humans' alteration of God's design for reproduction and the treatment of replicants as slave labor, the answer is a resounding *no*. As we know, however, God uses everything for the good of those who believe in Him, and the replicants ultimately point

---

[41] *Blade Runner 2049*, directed by Denis Villeneuve.

us back to questions about the morality of our behavior and our relationship with God.[42]

They also offer us a glimpse into the only family portrayed in either film. *BR* ends with Deckard leaving, if not for a happily ever after, at least for a chance of a relationship with another individual, Rachael. In *BR2049*, the replicants recognize life's inherent value more clearly than the humans and hail Deckard and Rachael's child as a "miracle."[43] Although this reaction can be partly attributed to Rachael's unknown ability to bear children, in their response, we also hear awe for life itself. The child is revealed to be Dr. Ana Stelline, whom we first meet in her laboratory, a kind of Eden filled with lush green plants. Of all the characters in either film, she comes closest to a Biblical approach of using her talents for the good of others in her creation of beautiful dream memories to be implanted in the replicants. She explains to K that although she cannot help or change the replicants' bleak futures, she can at least give them comforting memories. K praises her in his remark, "All the best memories are hers."[44]

---

[42] Rom. 8:28 (ESV).

[43] *Blade Runner 2049*, directed by Denis Villeneuve.

[44] Ibid.

At one point in the film, Deckard, Dr. Stelline's father, snaps at Niander Wallace, "I know what's real."[45] As Christians, we also know what is real: the importance of being made in the *imago Dei* and its resulting obligations on our lives to be good stewards of God's creation, our talents, and as we have seen here, most especially, our relationships. In losing our connection with God, we also lose our connection with each other. The two are inextricably linked, for when Jesus was asked what the greatest commandment was, He replied that it was to love the Lord our God but immediately added that the second was to love our neighbors as ourselves.[46] Indeed, "The human and the theological, in fact, are so intertwined that to speak authentically of one is to engage the other," and as Martin Buber points out, we must exist in being-in-relation with one another as subjects in an "I-Thou" relation.[47] [48]

Our relationships with God and each other are intertwined, and in placing our trust in Christ and

---

[45] *e Runner 2049*, directed by Denis Villeneuve.

[46] Robert K. Johnston, *Reel Spirituality: Theology and Film in Dialogue*, 2nd ed. (Grand Rapids: Baker Academic, 2006), 246.

[47] Ibid., 246-47.

[48] Ibid., 241.

restoring our relationship with Him, we can begin forging a path forward to bonding with others. Although our society has forgotten what it means to be a follower of Christ and thereby experience true human connection through Him, the ending of *BR2049* shows there is still hope for us. Even in so bleak a film, the story ends with a reunion of a father and daughter. If we believe in the potential of reunification of the natural family, how much more so should we look forward to that of our heavenly one with our brothers and sisters in Christ! — and how much harder should we work to show our society that a foretaste of it is possible here on earth when in communion with one another in the body of Christ?

When Deckard sees his daughter for the first time, Dr. Stelline is standing in a flurry of snow, letting the flakes fall onto her hand. "Beautiful, isn't it?" she asks.[49] Deckard approaches the laboratory and tentatively places his hand on the glass. We know what happens when we touch snow: it melts. As Lewis explains, we must participate with the triune God we serve if we are to heal the effects of sin and fulfill this essential aspect of our nature as created in the *imago Dei*:

---

[49] *Blade Runner 2049*, directed by Denis Villeneuve.

The whole dance, or drama, or pattern of this three-Personal life is to be played out in each one of us: or (putting it the other way round) each one of us has got to enter that pattern, take his place in that dance. There is no other way to the happiness for which we were made. Good things as well as bad, you know, are caught by a kind of infection. If you want to get warm you must stand near the fire: if you want to be wet you must get into the water. . . . Once a man is united to God, how could he not live forever? Once a man is separated from God, what can he do but wither and die?[50]

As Christians, we must not fear the flames or shy away from the water. We must take our places in the divine dance with the Father, the Son, and the Holy Spirit, and thereby with our neighbors to heal our broken, lonely lives and our broken, lonely world. Just as Dr. Stelline reaches for the snowflakes and Deckard reaches for his daughter's hand, we can begin thawing the coldness in our world, one relationship at a time.

And through Christ, it *will* be beautiful — won't it?

---

[50] Lewis, *Mere Christianity*, 176.

THORIN AND BILBO: IMAGE BEARERS

John L. Weitzel on Heroism, the Old Testament, and God's Will

Introduction

Literary characters such as those found in J.R.R. Tolkien's *The Hobbit* often reflects what is best in human nature or what Christians refer to as the divine stamp or *imago Dei*.[1] This essay will examine Thorin Oakenshield, the dwarf king, and Bilbo Baggins, the hobbit, as a king and prophet respectively, similar to ones found in the Jewish Scriptures, as told by J.R.R. Tolkien in his book *The Hobbit*.[2] Tolkien, an image-bearer and sub-creator, spent time crafting relatable and genuine characters. Thorin and Bilbo are bearers of the divine image and throughout the tale demonstrate

---

[1] In Genesis 1:26-27, male and female were created in the image of God, or imago Dei.

[2] Although a major motion picture was created using themes from this text, this essay analyzes the characters in the book and not the movie.

this by using the gifts God gave them in communion with each other. As Tolkien argues, one of the virtues of fairy stories is "to hold communion with other living things."[3] Gandalf, a wizard of the Istari order, designed their meeting in a humble abode in the Shire, in order to accomplish an important task. Noted Tolkien scholar Bradley Birzer, wrote that Gandalf is "the archetypal prefiguration of a powerful Prophet or Patriarch, a seer who beholds a vision of the Kingdom beyond the understanding of men."[4] Gandalf perceived that as each individual has at least one gift from the creator Eru (or in New Testament language the Holy Spirit), so each of these characters, bearing the image of God, has a particular gift and role to play in bringing about the will of the divine creator of Middle-earth.[5] Thorin is in many ways like the kings of Israel, and Bilbo is much like a prophet, and each is under the watchful eye of Gandalf, the Middle-earth version of an

---

[3] J.R.R. Tolkien, *On Fairy Stories* (London: Oxford University Press, 1939) 5.

[4] Bradley Birzer, *J.R.R. Tolkien's Sanctifying Myth* (Delaware: ISI Books, 2009) xii.

[5] For gifts of the Holy Spirit, see, for example, 1 Corinthians 12. All scriptural texts are from the English Standard Version (ESV).

angelic guide.[6]   Joseph Campbell, a professor of comparative mythology, identifies two types of heroic acts including "a courageous act in battle . . . the other kind is spiritual . . . (which) learns to experience the supernormal range of human spiritual life."[7] Along with a troop of twelve other dwarves and Gandalf, Thorin and Bilbo set out on an adventure to reenter the dwarven paradisiacal homeland and discover the true meaning of bearing God's image. Like several of the biblical kings of old, Thorin becomes a hero in the courageous act in battle sense, and the hobbit becomes a hero in the spiritual sense like the prophets of Israel.

Bilbo's gifts are faith and prophecy as he demonstrates endurance and motivation when things become difficult. Also, he is able to speak the truth, a type of wisdom, which he has received from Gandalf — a representative of God — to the king. Thorin's gift is knowledge, leadership, vision, and he is aware of everyone's roles and capabilities. Bilbo

---

[6] For more on priest, prophet, and king roles in Tolkien's work see Clyde S. Kilby, *Tolkien and* The Silmarillion (Wheaton, IL: Harold Shaw, 1976) 55-56. Also see, Birzer, *Sanctifying Myth*, 69-70. Kilby admits that Tolkien did not intend to use this imagery but found it appealing when introduced by Professor Barry Gordon in a 1967 presentation.

[7] Joseph Campbell, *The Power of Myth* (New York: Anchor Books, 1991) 151.

executed his gifts by using his heart and emotional fortitude, that is compassion. The hobbit remembers the beauty of the Shire and reminds the king of his vision, a promised land flowing with gold and freedom. Thorin executed his gifts through the use of reason and decisiveness. Each showed courage and the ability to communicate with each other and come to joint decisions, for the most part. C. S. Lewis, a scholar and friend of Tolkien, identifies courage as foundational to a virtuous life, "Courage is not simply one of the virtues but the form of every virtue at the testing point, which means at the point of highest reality."[8]

Although there are several similarities between certain Israelite prophets and kings, such as the prophet Jonah and King David, the Middle-earth duo most strikingly parallel the story of the Prophet Haggai and King Zerubbabel. This prophet likely traveled with the king and the Jewish people out of exile from Babylon, toward the city of Jerusalem which lay in ruins. Like Bilbo, Haggai encouraged the people to be strong and "fear not" and carried a signet ring which he would give to the king as a sign of his rule (though in *The Hobbit* the Ring has a very

---

[8] C.S. Lewis, *Screwtape Letters* (New York: Harper One, 1996), 161.

different meaning).[9] Likewise, the King Zerubbabel and Thorin have several interesting parallels in their histories and lives. Zerubbabel, like Thorin, is the grandson of the last active king in his homeland before their exile. They both had domestic issues when they arrived at their destination: destruction of the city and a dragon laying in wait respectively. Each had squabbles with local residents, as well. For example compare this verse from Ezra 4:3b, "You have nothing to do with us in building a house to our God" and Thorin's similar statement to Bard of Lake-town and the wood-elves, "To the treasure of my people no man has a claim, because Smaug who stole it from us also robbed him of life or home."[10] While the Babylonians destroyed the First Temple and the City of Jerusalem, the dragon had ruined the home of Thorin's kin, the Lonely Mountain. Both kings initially desired to exclude certain people groups from the restoration of their homeland. In each case, the prophet encouraged the king to act righteously at the appropriate time.

Let us now consider in detail how Bilbo used his image-bearing gifts in the way of the various

---

[9] Haggai 2:23.

[10] J.R.R. Tolkien, *The Hobbit* (Boston, First Mariner Books, 2012) 241-242.

prophets and Thorin in the way of several kings in the Jewish Scriptures. Each character in the saga, as with each one of us, are made in God's image. We have the potential to serve as priest, prophet, and king or queen, given to us at baptism.[11] Aligning one's will to the will of God, establishes an eternal relationship with the divine which culminates in union with God in the afterlife.

Prophet and King

The saga begins with the fifteen adventurers supping at Bilbo's dwelling and discussing their collective vision as well as the purpose of the hobbit, calling him the burglar or *"Expert Treasure-hunter."*[12] It is important to note that this burglary was a reclamation of stolen property and land by a notorious creature, the dragon Smaug, and not an actual theft. As all good adventures ought, this one begins with song and merriment. This is reminiscent of the song of the Valar from Tolkien's *The Silmarillion*, where he writes "In this Music the World was begun; for Iluvatar made visible the song

---

[11] See 1 Peter 2:9-10.

[12] Tolkien, *The Hobbit*, 241-242. Also, note the importance of sharing a meal together. Passover, showing hospitality (e.g. Gen. 18:4-5), Jesus feeding the thousands, and Last Supper/Eucharist are examples.

of the Ainur, and they beheld it was a light in the darkness."[13] Jonathan S. McIntosh, describing Tolkien's world, notes that, "Music is the part of world-history containing the creation and consequent free choices of the 'incarnate intelligences' of Elves and Men."[14] Indeed the dwarves and company were continuing the song, for those who set their sights on evil do not sing such songs nor enjoy merriment of any kind. Tolkien writes, "As they sang the hobbit felt the love of beautiful things made by hands, and by cunning and by magic moving through him, a fierce and a jealous love, the desire of the hearts of dwarves."[15] This recognition of appreciating beauty will serve Bilbo well as he gains confidence as a prophet. The giftedness of the dwarves was in the creation of things which continues the creative instinct of those who bear the image of God. This is an example of Tolkien's sub-creation motif; Birzer explains that Tolkien thought that each person is a "subcreator

---

[13] Tolkien, *The Silmarillion* (New York, Ballantine Books, 1999) 15.

[14] Jonathan S. McIntosh, *The Flame Imperishable: Tolkien, St. Thomas, and the Metaphysics of Fairie* (New York: Angelico Press, 2018) 60. See also his section on "Ainulindalë *and the* Musica Universalis," 119-127.

[15] Tolkien, *The Hobbit*, 16.

made in the image of the true creator. God places each uniquely created individual in a certain time, in a certain place, and with certain gifts, for a certain reason."[16]

Not every dwarf believed in Bilbo, but Gandalf reminded them that he had called him out or chosen him for a grand purpose because of his remarkable gift as an image-bearer.[17] In accepting his role, Bilbo took on a challenge of both a journey out into the world as well as an inner journey into his very soul. Gandalf articulates his decision to select Bilbo by proclaiming, "There is a lot more in him than you guess, and a deal more than he has any idea of himself."[18] Bilbo would follow his heart, at times become the actual leader of the group, advise the king, and challenge him — thus fulfilling the role of prophet. Compare Bilbo here to the prophet Jonah who knew what he was called to do but was often reluctant and eventually entered Nineveh and convinced the king and the people to repent.[19]

---

[16] Birzer, *Sanctifying Myth*, 110.

[17] See Ephesians 1:4-5, even as he chose us in him before the foundation of the world, that we should be holy and blameless before him. In love he predestined us for adoption to himself as sons through Jesus Christ, according to the purpose of his will. All scriptural texts are from the English Standard Version (ESV).

[18] Tolkien, *The Hobbit*, 19.

[19] See Jonah 3.

Thorin, for his part, articulated his vision of the venture, to seek out their fatherland where even the poorest "had money to spend and to lend, and leisure to make beautiful things, just for the fun of it, not to speak of the most marvelous and magical toys."[20] As a leader he had great vision and the respect of his fellow dwarves who saw him as both a reminder of their valiant past and hope for a bright future. Thorin, like King David, held his people together and desired to defeat whatever enemy was at his doorstep. This duo was participating in God's grace through their collective effort as image-bearers who are using their gifts for the benefit of all. Participation in grace flows from God in the natural and ordinary way people operate, as Thomas Aquinas writes, it is "our intellect (which) knows some things naturally; thus the first principles of the intelligibles, whose intelligible conceptions-called interior words-naturally exist in the intellect and proceed from it."[21] Both image-bearers had a predisposition to the good, which flowed from reason, despite the fact that they occasionally succumbed to the bad. This is the traditional view of

---

[20] Tolkien, *The Hobbit*, 22.

[21] Thomas Aquinas, *Summa Contra Gentiles*, Book Four: Salvation, trans. Charles J. O'Neil (Notre Dame: University of Notre Dame Press, 1975) IV.11.17.

morality as Lewis discusses in his *Discarded Image* where he argues that "Moral imperatives therefore were uttered by Reason."[22]

The adventure to recover the lost treasure, protected by the dragon Smaug, is set in a wider story. To those who could read the signs of the times, a darkness was spreading throughout Middle-earth. Most of the troop was not aware of the significance of the return of the dragons and the spread of the goblins since the battle of the Mines of Moria. Gandalf "knew how evil and danger had grown and thriven in the Wild."[23] These goblins were "cruel, wicked, and bad hearted. They make no beautiful things, but they make clever ones."[24] When the troop ventured into the goblins' cavern in the Misty Mountains, they came upon those who held a "special grudge against Thorin's people."[25] Called by Gandalf to use his ancient sword, Thorin was fulfilling his role as king and protector of his people, using his gifts of leadership and courage.[26]

---

[22] C.S. Lewis, *The Discarded Image: An Introduction to Medieval and Renaissance Literature* (London: Cambridge University Press, 1964) 159.

[23] Tolkien, *The Hobbit*, 53.

[24] Ibid., 59.

[25] Ibid.

[26] Ibid., 63.

After getting separated from the group as they battled the goblins, Bilbo awoke in a dark and tight place deep beneath the mountain. Here he had a choice to sink into darkness or use his God-given gifts to emerge as a messenger of faith. As he crawled he discovered a "tiny ring of cold metal lying on the floor of the tunnel."[27] He put the ring in his pocket not knowing its history nor the destiny of the magical object. Tolkien describes the hobbit here as one possessing "a fund of wisdom and wise sayings that men have mostly never heard or have forgotten long ago."[28] This cognitive ability coupled with wisdom would come in handy soon. He pressed forward with his sword in hand and some hope in his heart. Soon he would come across another creature who was the owner of this Ring for 478 years. This creature was Sméagol, better known as Gollum.

They met near the underground lake beneath the dark mountain. The only chance for Bilbo to escape this place and try to find his companions would be with the help of this creature. "Gollum had not actually threatened to kill him, or tried to yet.

---

[27] Tolkien, *The Hobbit*, 65.

[28] Ibid., 66.

And he was miserable, alone, lost."[29] Here Bilbo's true character of compassion or emotional-fortitude, a hallmark of *imago Dei*, emerged when a "sudden understanding, a pity mixed with horror, welled up in Bilbo's heart: a glimpse of endless unmarked days without light or hope of betterment."[30] This Ring allowed him to outwit the formidable Gollum in a game of riddles, as if it was destined for Bilbo to not only find it but allow him to escape. The ability to wear this Ring without succumbing to its evils is a testament to his role as prophet.[31]

The dwarves in the meantime were not out of danger. They were being pursued by the goblins from the mountain. Thorin had them hidden for a time. Bilbo happened upon them using his Ring to sneak in. Later the goblins chased them toward a cliff where the wizard, hobbit, and dwarves hid in the trees. The Lord of the Eagles of Misty Mountains noticed the troop from above and observed the wolves and goblins. Thanks to the handiwork of the

---

[29] Tolkien, *The Hobbit*, 81.

[30] Ibid.

[31] For more on the role of evil in Tolkien, and the ring in particular, see Peter J. Kreeft, *Philosophy of Tolkien* (San Francisco: Ignatius Press, 2005) 180-184.

wizard, they were able to set the trees on fire.[32] While the frightened wizard Gandalf taunted the goblins, the eagles swooped down and rescued them.[33] Courage, in the face of danger was the virtue which propelled them to safety.

It is here in the story that the role of prophet or guide was passed on to Bilbo by Gandalf, reminiscent of the prophet Elijah chosing Elisha as his successor.[34] Like Elijah blessed Elisha, Gandalf blesses the hobbit saying, "There are no safe paths in this part of the world . . . land of the Necromancer . . . keep your spirits up, hope for the best, and with a tremendous slice of luck you come out one day."[35] To the whole troop he bids them safe journey and farewell saying, "Good-bye! Be good, take care of yourselves – and DON'T LEAVE THE PATH!"[36]

For a time the king-prophet duo of Thorin and Bilbo would need to work together without the aid of the wizard. Here is where Bilbo, the prophet-in-

---

[32] Tolkien, *The Hobbit*, 96.

[33] Ibid., 98.

[34] See 2 Kings 2:9, When they had crossed, Elijah said to Elisha, "Ask what I shall do for you, before I am taken from you." And Elisha said, "Please let there be a double portion of your spirit on me."

[35] Tolkien, *The Hobbit*, 129.

[36] Ibid.

training, learns what it means to *have more about him than others know.* Thorin, aware of the roles and capabilities of his troop, does not seek advice from one of his fellow dwarves but from the new prophetic voice. Tolkien writes, "How far away do you think it is?" asked Thorin, for by now they knew Bilbo had the sharpest eyes among them."[37] The king and hobbit were definitely the leaders who relied on each other's skill and abilities to trek through the forest. The duo used their gifts and talents together as image-bearers for a grand purpose. "'Who'll cross first?' asked Bilbo. 'I shall,' said Thorin."[38] A peripatetic dialogue ensued between the two, serving them well until they reached the mountain and encountered the dragon. As they weaved their way through the forest the mood of one would shift from gloomy to hopeful while the other would experience the opposite. One would lift the spirit of the other.

Upon crossing an enchanted stream, the dwarf king, keeping true to his vision, "was the only one who had kept his feet and his wits."[39] Soon after they fell into despair. Though struggling along in

---

[37] Tolkien, *The Hobbit*, 132.

[38] Ibid., 133.

[39] Ibid., 134.

gloominess, the troop was so close to their destination that "if [only] they had kept up their courage and their hope, to thinner trees and places where the sunlight came again."[40] The hobbit-prophet had climbed a tree to see where they were; he did not have eyes to see their true location. Tolkien writes, "Actually, as I have told you, they were not far off the edge of the forest; and if Bilbo had had the sense to see it, the tree that he had climbed, though it was tall in itself, was standing near the bottom of a wide valley . . . he did not see this, and he climbed down full of despair."[41] The king, for his part, was beginning to lose his patience and was beginning to snap at those around him. The king's irritation began to grow here due to the long journey. As happens in every adventure, unnatural actions including evil can consume an individual for a time, for "life is a spiritual warfare."[42] But as will be seen, "obedience and duty come down to knowing, trusting, and loving a person," this is part of the duo's integral connection of *imago Dei*.[43]

---

[40] Tolkien, *The Hobbit*, 136.

[41] Ibid., 138.

[42] Kreeft, *The Philosophy of Tolkien,* 177.

[43] Ibid., 196.

Retreating as if to pray, as the prophet Elijah did in 1 Kings, Bilbo went to nap near a tree, "thinking of his far distant hobbit-hole with its beautiful pantries."[44] They were lost, despairing, and confused — their defenses were down, so danger took advantage. Since they had lost their vision, they walked right into spiderwebs. While trapped in the web, a great spider came at Bilbo, he drew out his sword and cut himself loose from the web "and stuck it with his sword right in the eyes."[45] Tolkien writes that, "Somehow the killing of the giant spider, all alone by himself in the dark without the help of the wizard or the dwarves or of anyone else, made a great difference to Mr. Baggins. He felt a different person, and much fiercer and bolder."[46] He called the sword Sting. This naming of the sword symbolizes his new found courage which begins the transformation of Bilbo becoming a spiritual hero and is an essential feature of *imago Dei* since only sentient beings name things. He fought off many spiders by throwing stones. Because of his newfound bravery, the dwarves saw a real hero

---

[44] Tolkien, *The Hobbit*, 143. See also 1 Kings 19:4-8.

[45] Ibid.

[46] Ibid., 144.

begin to emerge in the hobbit. Even "Knowing the truth about the vanishing did not lessen their opinion of Bilbo at all; for they saw that he had some wits, as well as luck and a magic ring."[47]

During a battle with the spiders, their king was taken by the wood-elves unbeknownst to the others, and panic ensued. They had lost their path and their leader. Thorin, as it turns out, was meeting with the elf-king who wanted a share of the money the dragon was hoarding. Since love of money is the root of all evil and Thorin loved money, the dwarf king was not willing to part with any part of his treasure; thus he was imprisoned.[48] Here the king did not rely on reason, forgot his vision of returning to his paradisiacal homeland, and was not showing hospitality. Like many of the kings of Israel, who were otherwise blessed by God, he succumbed to evil.

The rest of the dwarves were soon captured, and Bilbo followed them invisible with his Ring on. "I am like a burglar that can't get away," he said, "but must go on miserably burgling the same house day after

---

[47] Tolkien, *The Hobbit*, 153.

[48] See 1 Timothy 6:10 For the love of money is a root of all kinds of evils. It is through this craving that some have wandered away from the faith and pierced themselves with many pangs.

day . . . I wish I was back in my hobbit-hole."[49]
Tolkien tells us here that "if anything was to be done,
it would have to be done by Mr. Baggins, alone and
unaided."[50] Just as the king had sunken into despair,
even to the point of giving up some of his potential
wealth, Bilbo appeared. Tolkien writes, "Thorin was
too wretched to be angry any longer at his
misfortunes, and was even beginning to think of
telling the king all about his treasure and his quest
(which shows how low-spirited he had become),
when he heard Bilbo's little voice at his keyhole."[51]
Bilbo relayed the message to the other captured
dwarves that Thorin was also captured, but alive.
Again, their spirits were lifted by the action and
leadership of the hobbit and the patience of their
king. Tolkien writes,

> They all thought their own shares in the
> treasure . . . would suffer seriously if the
> Woodelves claimed part of it, and they all
> trusted Bilbo. Just what Gandalf had said
> would happen . . . Perhaps that was part of

---

[49] Tolkien, *The Hobbit,* 161.

[50] Ibid..

[51] Ibid.

his reason for going off and leaving them.[52]

The wizard needed to leave them to their own devices so that they would grow as a community or nation, flowing from the leadership of the king and hobbit.

Bilbo's wisdom and courage enabled him to make quick decisions that saved the lives of the dwarves whom the wizard entrusted to him. Having the keys to the jail cells, Bilbo commands, "No time now! . . . you just follow me! We must all keep together and not risk getting separated."[53] Here is the strongest use of prophetic voice for Bilbo. At first the dwarves were uncertain about climbing into the barrels and being dumped over the waterfall. However, the king assumed his leadership role saying, "Upon my word! . . . Gandalf spoke true, as usual! A pretty fine burglar you make, it seems, when the time comes."[54]

As they sped on their way they caught a glimpse of their final destination. The "Mountain seemed to frown at him and threaten him as it drew ever

---

[52] Tolkien, *The Hobbit,* 162.

[53] Ibid., 164.

[54] Ibid., 165.

nearer."[55] It was a perilous journey on the river, but soon they landed near Lake-town. Some of the dwarves were a bit moody about it. Using his prophetic gift of motivation, he reminded them of the king's vision, as Tolkien relays,

> Bilbo asking quite crossly, "are you alive or dead? . . . Are you still in prison, or are you free? If you want food, and if you want to go on with this silly adventure-it's yours after all and not mine-you had better slap your arms and rub your legs and try to help me get the others out while there is still a chance."[56]

Tolkien tells us that "Thorin of course saw the sense of this."[57] Then Thorin congratulates Bilbo, "And I suppose we ought to thank our stars and Mr. Baggins. I am sure he has a right to expect it, though I wish he could have arranged a more comfortable journey."[58] Thorin greets the Master of the town, introducing himself as Thorin son of Thrain son of Thror King under the Mountain.[59] The crowds sang

---

[55] Tolkien, *The Hobbit*, 175.

[56] Ibid., 178-179.

[57] Ibid., 179.

[58] Ibid.

[59] Ibid., 181.

songs both old and new. "Thorin looked and walked as if his kingdom was already regained and Smaug chopped up into little pieces,"[60] as if walking in the presence of God. "Then, as he had said, the dwarves' good feeling towards the little hobbit grew stronger every day."[61] Here Thorin and Bilbo show their partnership as king and prophet, melding together their calling, and using their gifts as an *imago Dei* duo most strongly.

In this part of the adventure, the moods of the group began to ebb and flow. From gloomy to hopeful and back to gloomy, again, the dwarves and Bilbo were continually at odds.[62] This is a microcosm of living in a fallen world and mirrors the history of the nation of Israel who at times were in line with God's purpose and at times were not. Even though all are created in the image of God and have gifts from the divine, the day to day life is not without its challenges. The prophet's duty is keeping faith, and if that fails, then the team fails. The king's duty is to hold on to the vision, for if he loses sight of that, then they lose their way. Bilbo thought, "It is always poor me that has to get them

---

[60] Tolkien, *The Hobbit,* 183.

[61] Ibid.

[62] Ibid., 185-192.

out of their difficulties, at least since the wizard left."[63] They found themselves at the secret door where the key hole appears at the last light of the sun on Durin's Day. Because of the thrush, Bilbo was able to see the keyhole that everyone else thought was missed. ""The key! The key!" cried Bilbo. "Where is Thorin?" . . . Thorin stepped up and drew the key on its chain from round his neck."[64] The lot of them pushed the door open and entered the halls of the mountain. Thorin spoke, "Now is the time for our esteemed Mr. Baggins, who has proved himself a good companion on our long road, and a hobbit full of courage and resource far exceeding his size."[65] When the king remembers his role to provide leadership, holds on to the vision of the quest, and communicates with his hobbit-prophet, then things begin to go well.

Tolkien writes that "he was a very different hobbit from the one that had runout without a pocket-handkerchief from Bag-End long ago."[66] Here was the moment of his calling, to seek what was lost many years prior, to go and face a dragon,

---

[63] Tolkien, *The Hobbit*, 193.

[64] Ibid., 194.

[65] Ibid., 195.

[66] Ibid., 196.

not as a knight but as a prophet seeking beauty from a fallen place. "It was at this point that Bilbo stopped. Going on from there was the bravest thing he ever did."[67] He dragged out a two-handled cup from the dragon's lair. It was a momentous time for the dwarves to pass around a sample of the treasure. They heard the dragon awaken and they wanted to escape the mountain. The king then had to play his part deciding to stay and distract the dragon since two dwarves were outside defenseless tending to the ponies and supplies. ""Nonsense!" said Thorin, recovering his dignity. "We cannot leave them. Get inside Mr. Baggins and Balin.""[68] Knowledge and courage predominated the king's thoughts at this moment.

The dragon came to hunt down the thieves who stole from him. Bilbo begged them to do something about the dragon but the dwarves were frightened of such a conundrum. The king nobly requested the advice of his prophet-hobbit by asking, "What then do you propose we should do, Mr. Baggins?"[69] Bilbo responded, "Personally I have no hopes at all, and

---

[67] Tolkien, *The Hobbit,* 197.

[68] Ibid., 200.

[69] Ibid., 202.

wish I was safe back at home."[70] However, knowing what needed to be done and in an act of faith, Bilbo volunteered to put on his Ring and go see what the dragon was up to. He said, "'Every worm has his weak spot.'" Naturally the dwarves accepted the offer eagerly. "Now he had become the real leader in their adventure."[71] In Jewish Scriptures, the hierarchy of society is God then prophet then king. Bilbo here, reminiscent of Jonah the reluctant prophet, takes his role to the next level by taking to heart his call. True compassion is acting for the sake of others even when one does not feel like it. This is an example of living out one's image of God.

Bilbo finds and speaks to Smaug, "I did not come for presents. I only wished to have a look at you and see if you were truly as great as tales say."[72] Bilbo notices a gap in the dragon's armor that would serve as useful information. Thorin, Bilbo, and the others were discussing what the best strategy was in dealing with the dragon. "You are very gloomy, Mr. Baggins!" said Thorin.[73] "We knew it would be a

---

[70] Tolkien, *The Hobbit,* 203.

[71] Ibid.

[72] Ibid., 204.

[73] Ibid., 211.

desperate venture," said Thorin. Center on the king's mind was the Arkenstone, the prize of dwarven kings. "But somehow, just when the dwarves were most despairing, Bilbo felt a strange lightening of the heart, as if a heavy weight had gone from under his waistcoat."[74] He said, "While there's life there's hope!"[75] The search for treasure began by the team. "In desperation they agreed, and Thorin was the first to go forward by Bilbo's side."[76] Tolkien reiterated that the dwarves proclaimed that "Mr. Baggins was still officially their expert burglar and investigator."[77] When the nation of Israel recognized and listened to God's prophet, prosperity was not far behind.

Bilbo found and pocketed the Arkenstone, unsure if he wanted to reveal it to the king just yet. Deep in the cavern was panic as the dwarves gathered the treasure. Bilbo exclaimed, ""The light's gone out! Someone come and find and help me!" For the moment his courage had failed altogether."[78] Thorin commanded however, "It seems we have got

---

[74] Tolkien, *The Hobbit*, 214.

[75] Ibid.

[76] Ibid., 215.

[77] Ibid., 216.

[78] Ibid., 218.

to go and help our burglar."[79] Watching the dwarves enjoy a bit too much their found treasure, "Mr. Baggins kept his head more clear of the bewitchment of the hoard than the dwarves did."[80] Note that the lights go out and bewitchment enters onto the scene, which then leads to love of money becoming dominant rather than brotherhood.

Again, a peripatetic dialogue between Bilbo and Thorin served them well as they sought the best strategy for getting past a watchful Smaug. Bilbo spoke to Thorin,

> "We are armed, but what good has any armour ever been before against Smaug the Dreadful? This treasure is not won back yet."[81]

> "You speak the truth!" answered Thorin, recovering his wits, "Let us go! I will guide you."[82]

> "'Come, come!" said Thorin laughing-his spirits had begun to rise again, and he rattled the precious stones in his pockets . . . Don't call my palace a nasty hole! You

---

[79] Tolkien, *The Hobbit*, 218.

[80] Ibid., 219.

[81] Ibid., 219.

[82] Ibid., 220.

wait till it has been cleaned and
redecorated!'

'That won't be till Smaug's dead,' said
Bilbo."[83]

In this dialogue they come to an agreement about
what needs to be done now and defines hope for the
future.

Smaug was killed in Lake-town by Bard the
Bowman. A wise raven informed Thorin to trust
Bard and not the Master of the Lake-men. There was
an attempted parley between Bard and Thorin, but
the king was stubborn. Bilbo's concern was justice,
but Thorin's was vengeance.[84] Bilbo delivered the
Arkenstone to Bard. Bilbo identifies the Arkenstone
as the heart of the king, as well as of the mountain.[85]
At this moment Thorin's heart was hardened and he
did not act as one who bore the image of God.
Gandalf had returned and remarked, "Well done! Mr.
Baggins! . . . there is always more about you than
anyone expects."[86] Bilbo returned to the mountain
to be with the dwarves. Bard held aloft the
Arkenstone of Thrain for Thorin to see. Bilbo admits

---

[83] Tolkien, *The Hobbit*, 222.

[84] Ibid., 241.

[85] Ibid., 248.

[86] Ibid., 249.

to Thorin that he gave the Arkenstone away. Thorin threatened to toss Bilbo over the rocks"[87] Gandalf appeared and asked for no harm to come to his burglar. Bilbo exclaimed that he took it as part of his fourteenth share. Thorin exclaims that he is betrayed by a traitor. "You are not making a very splendid figure as King under the Mountain," said Gandalf.[88] Often in the Jewish Scriptures, the king failed to listen to God's prophet.

During this tumultuous time, there did not seem to be a solution to despair. Something dramatic would have to happen to bring everyone together. Suddenly they hear, "The Goblins are upon you!" Gandalf cried.[89] Tolkien writes,

> "So began a battle that none had expected; and it was called the Battle of the Five Armies . . . Goblins and the Wild Wolves . . . Elves and Men and Dwarves."[90]

> "Thorin wielded his axe with mighty strokes, and nothing seemed to harm him . . . Thorin drove right against the

---

[87] Tolkien, *The Hobbit*, 252.

[88] Ibid.

[89] Ibid., 255.

[90] Ibid., 256.

bodyguard of Bolg. But he could not pierce their ranks."[91]

The Eagles came to help the team for the second time. Thorin's courageous decision to engage in battle rather than hold up in his cavernous home, is his climatic arc in the saga. Like most of the kings of Israel, showing leadership on the battlefield is a hallmark of fulfilling God's plan in establishing and defending the promised land.

Bilbo had been hit in the head during the fighting and was carried back to camp and went in to see Thorin who had suffered a fatal injury. King Thorin, like King David, both accomplished his God-given purpose but also sinned. In the end, however, he reconciled with one he sinned against.

> "Farewell, good thief," he said. "I go now to the halls of waiting to sit beside my fathers, until the world is renewed."[92]

> "I wish to part in friendship with you, and I would take back my words and deeds at the Gate."[93]

---

[91] Tolkien, *The Hobbit*, 259.

[92] Ibid., 262.

[93] Ibid.

The king, like David, confessed his sins and asked for forgiveness.

> Bilbo knelt on one knee filled with sorrow. "Farewell, King under the Mountain!" he said. "This is a bitter adventure, if it must end so; and not a mountain of gold can amend it."[94]

> "I am glad that I have shared in your perils-that has been more than any Baggins deserves."[95]

Thorin acknowledges that the prophet fulfilled his role, while Bilbo accepts his apology. "No!" said Thorin. "There is more in you of good than you know, child of the kindly West. Some courage and some wisdom, blended in measure."[96]

It was time for Bilbo to return home. After the goodbyes he made sure to invite them to stop by at any time and reminded them that tea-time was 4:00 PM.

The duo of Thorin and Bilbo set out on an adventure along with a troop of twelve other dwarves and the wizard to reenter the dwarven paradisiacal homeland and discover the true

---

[94] Tolkien, *The Hobbit*, 262.

[95] Ibid., 263.

[96] Ibid.

meaning of bearing God's image. Gandalf articulates his decision to select Bilbo by saying, "There is a lot more in him than you guess, and a deal more than he has any idea of himself."[97]

Conclusion

Each human is created in the image and likeness of God. Every individual has the potential to act as priest, prophet, and king or queen. To do so requires one to align one's will with God, as Bilbo and Thorin did in *The Hobbit*. Gandalf, an agent of the divine not unlike an angel of the Lord in the Jewish Scriptures, calls out Bilbo to go on a special mission. Like Jonah he reluctantly goes and finds that his soul is challenged and his body is battered by the experience. Like Haggai he is able to forge an alliance and partnership with the king to do what is right in the eyes of God. During his physical journey he also goes on an inner spiritual journey and uses his gifts of wisdom and faith to become a leader of the troop. Along the way he discovers a magic Ring that will one day lead to the destruction of an evil that is already growing in the land. Some of the prophetic motifs that play out in Bilbo's story and prove his image-bearing nature include his emotional

---

[97] Tolkien, *The Hobbit*, 19.

fortitude, reclamation of stolen property -- that is -- restoration, compassion, keen eyes, standing up to the king as Nathan did to David in 2 Samuel 2, and lifting other's spirits even when his spirits were gloomy. Finally, he caused the 'lights to go back on' in the heart of Thorin, for as Bilbo exclaimed in prophetic fashion, "while there is life, there is hope!"[98] The hobbit fulfilled Campbell's definition of a spiritual hero.

Thorin, like King David, is a mighty and courageous warrior who protects his people and defends their honor. He also desires to build a kingdom. Like King Zerubbabel, he needs to overcome several obstacles including a devastated homeland and a fractious people. Thorin uses his gifts of knowledge to lead his people toward a specific goal with courage and fortitude. He also overcomes his lust for gold and the Arkenstone to find what it really means to be an image-bearer. Friendship, camaraderie, and righteousness are far more valuable than treasure. He discovers that a hobbit is as trustworthy and wise as a wizard. Some of the kingly motifs that are part of Thorin's story include use of reason, laying out a purpose for their venture, seeking out the promised land, vision and

---

[98] Tolkien, *The Hobbit,* p. 214.

understanding of their valiant path, protector and defender, seeking wise counsel, patience, recognizing others for their heroism, speaking to other leaders, displaying confidence, apologizing for misdeeds, and making amends. The king fulfilled Campbell's definition of the courageous hero.

Birzer says that part of Tolkien's legacy is his emphasis on using our gifts as persons created in God's image, in the "service of the betterment of our selves, our community, our society, the Church, and, ultimately the world."[99] In other words, each person has a responsibility of using their gifts, not simply for developing their own ego, but in service to others. Thorin and Bilbo's peripatetic dialectic approach to shared leadership is an example of the proper function of being an image-bearer. The team of dwarves could not have made it to Lonely Mountain without both their king's gifts of knowledge and courage as well as Bilbo's gifts of wisdom and faith. This realization speaks of a eucatastrophe, a neologism coined by Tolkien in his essay, *On Fairy-stories* to describe the literary device of the "happy ending."[100] In the end each character found his resting place. For Thorin this was dying a

---

[99] Birzer, *Sanctifying Myth*, 136.

[100] McIntosh, *Flame Imperishable*, 63.

hero and his spirit traveling to lay with his fathers and for Bilbo, it was going home to enjoy beauty and rest from his adventures. By using one's gift in service of others, that is recognizing that we are created in God's image, "the journey of sanctification begins," as Birzer notes.[101] This is the true meaning of being image bearers. The restoration of the hobbit to the beauty of the Shire and the king to the beauty of not only his promised land but ultimately his heavenly home, is the penultimate meaning of life.

---

[101] Birzer, *Sanctifying Myth*, 70.

Deepest Wonder, Remarkable Beauty: Sonnets in Praise of Life and the Imago Dei

Annie Nardone on the Miracle of Life

We have come to a time when our culture craves autonomy – to an extreme. Not only are we divided from our neighbors, but we have also severed one of the most fundamental human bonds of all: the emotional connection between mother and child. A preborn baby can be compartmentalized as a problem that can be easily solved by termination. Our apologetic effort to illuminate the fact that this child is like no other and alive from the first moments of conception needs to extend to society as a whole, changing the perspective to see life as an astounding miracle and each child created in the image of the Creator.

Author Malcolm Guite notes that in poetry "our vision is doubled; we become aware simultaneously both of the word as a thing in itself, a chosen sound, a kind of music in the air, and also of that other reality, that mystery of truth of which the word is the gatekeeper."[1] Poetry emotionally connects the reader to the message, and it sets aside the rhetoric of the abortion debate, pointing to the remarkable beauty of life by focusing on conception and the preborn baby.

There are several reasons why poetry is a beautiful method to help people see life in a fresh way. First, poetry can combat the loss of meaning in our words. Holly Ordway, Fellow of Faith and Culture, Word on Fire Institute, states that we must do "the difficult work of meaning-making in our Christian apologetics, we must also fight against the distortion of language."[2] Poetry is written with carefully chosen words imbued with meaning and condensed into rhythm and rhyme that appeal to our imagination.

Poetry also works as a narrative to help our imaginations perceive an idea in a personal way, in contrast to reading a laundry list of scientific statements. As human beings created in the likeness of God, "we have an innate need for meaning in our

---

[1] Malcolm Guite, *Faith, Hope and Poetry* (London: Routledge, 2012), 160.

[2] Holly Ordway, *Apologetics and the Christian Imagination* (Steubenville, OH: Emmaus Road, 2017), 59.

lives. Because we are creatures who inhabit time and — importantly — who perceive the passing of time, we need to have this meaning expressed in a fundamentally narrative form."[3] Readers may connect meaningfully to a sonnet sequence that spans actual, human time and reads as a narrative form. In other words, these sonnets are explaining to the mother, "This is your life and the life of your baby in the next few months. You already have a relationship even before you look into each other's eyes." This baby is part of the mother's story, and because we are "naturally predisposed to take in truth in the form of a narrative," this truth naturally works as an imaginative work of literature.[4]

We can approach the pro-life issue from a different perspective and take a closer look at the development of a baby in the womb as a poetic theme. Facts are important so that we can effectively respond to pro-choice arguments like, "The fetus is literally a part of the pregnant woman," and questions regarding the "viability" of the baby.[5] Surprisingly, it is very difficult to get a

---

[3] Ordway, *Apologetics.*, 102-103.

[4] Ibid., 103.

[5] David Hershenov, "Ten (Bad, But Popular) Arguments for Abortion," *Public Discourse*, August 23, 2017, accessed March 6, 2019, https://www.thepublicdiscourse.com/2017/08/19718/.

straightforward, true, and detailed answer. Lila Rose, president of pro-life organization Live Action, directed me to websites that broke down the developmental stages into days rather than months.[6] I am convinced that if people knew the miracles in each stage of development, hearts would be turning to cherish life. The following sonnets include many details of fetal development to leave a lasting image.

The pro-life and pro-choice debate has continued for so long that we have lost the true meaning of human life. Arguments have been reduced to repeated slogans, and we lay down words like children playing cards, always trying to trump each other with a clever play. Ordway states that "dialogue is often reduced to shouting slogans back and forth (a problem not limited to religious dialogue, to be sure)."[7] The clichés no longer mean anything. Meanwhile, abortions continue because the culture fails to comprehend that every child in the abortion debate is a miracle. Relying on reason alone has shown itself to be a weak method to affect hearts and minds. The missing component is

---

[6] "The Endowment for Human Development," *The Endowment for Human Development*, accessed March 5, 2019, http://www.ehd.org .

[7] Ordway, *Apologetics.*, 21.

imagination awakened by literature, and especially poetry.

An argument for abortion is that the baby is not actually a person until after it is born and any rights the baby is entitled to are bestowed well after birth. Before birth, and even for a time after birth, the child is merely a creature without rights according to the standards of Peter Singer, Professor of Bioethics, Princeton University and Laureate Professor of Applied Philosophy and Public Ethics, University of Melbourne. In his book *Writings on an Ethical Life*, Singer writes, "If the fetus does not have the same claim to life as a person, it appears that the newborn baby does not either, and the life of a newborn baby is of less value to it than the life of a pig, a dog, or a chimpanzee is to the nonhuman animal."[8] Christopher Kaczor writes, "If it can be shown that personhood begins sometime after birth, it will be all the more evident that personhood does not begin prior to birth, and so abortion is not morally wrong."[9] We become embroiled in straw-man arguments over terms like *fetus*, *human*, and *person*. This is dangerous ground to tread because fetal

---

[8] Peter Singer, *Writings on an Ethical Life* (New York: Ecco Press, 2000), 160-161.

[9] Christopher Kaczor, *The Ethics of Abortion* (New York: Routledge, 2011), 13.

development is left to interpretation of terms. Science proves that life starts with two cells combining to form a unique set of DNA markers. These markers are the guiding plan in forming a new, unique human being, regardless of the label we would attach to him or her. Labels can dehumanize and keep us comfortably alienated from the truth.

Because we dislike inconvenience and emotional pain, a baby with a limited life span is viewed by society to have little worth. In fact, it is easy to consider them a burden to society and to the family. The solution to the 'problem' has been abortion for a variety of reasons — we wonder what kind of life will this child have? Many believe that since the baby will die anyhow, let's just put it out of its misery now. 'Quality of life' is a phrase that factors into the decision of abortion and we think that any child who is not born normal (but what is normal and by whose standards?) could not possibly be happy and successful. This attitude comes frightfully close to Darwin's atheistic view of natural selection. He believed in the "idea of impersonal, random chance guiding the development of species" and survival of the fittest with the "death of the 'unfit' resulting in the overall population becoming 'better'."[10] Therefore, the unfit are not worthy of life or deserving of a chance. In a dystopian twist, society is advanced by the elimination of the imperfect, but by what standard do we conclude that someone has worth?

My family has personal experience with our baby who had "life-limiting" circumstances, and I have always felt God's call to use that difficult pregnancy to encourage other families. Dr. Elvira Parravicini, neonatologist at Morgan Stanley's Children's Hospital, wrote an inspiring article about caring for babies who were not expected to survive. Rather than seeing these babies as a hopeless medical situation, she treated each one as a patient in need of "comfort care." She believes that doctors should be "creative, using all our medical knowledge and our humanity."[11] This respect for life recognizes the humanity of the child in a way the false solution of abortion cannot do.

I carried our daughter until she died at seven months gestation as a result of her "life-limiting" condition. She has always been a beloved and valued

---

[10] Holly Ordway, "Lecture Notes, Unit 1B" (Lecture, Houston Baptist University, Houston, TX, January 14, 2019).

[11] Elvira Parravicini, M.D., "Aspects of Beauty: The Medical Care of Terminally Ill Newborns," *Humanum* 1, no. 1 (2014), accessed March 5, 2019, http://humanumreview.com/articles/aspects-of-beauty-the-medical-care-of-terminally-ill-newborns .

member of our family, and our relationship with her wasn't cut short by abortion. The impact of her brief life on our family started a ripple effect of blessing on hundreds of people and continues thirteen years after her death. She had a tiny 'narrative': conception, life, and death in a little over seven months, but her earthly story is complete, and we loved her through her life, bringing closure to our grief.

Poetic language can beautifully speak meaning into a sensitive issue. I wrote the following sonnets to resonate the abiding and purposeful love which God created both the universe's expanse and each tiny human life, declaring all of His creation good. The sonnet "Creation" uses a macrocosm and microcosm comparing the universe to a tiny child to symbolize this idea. The three-sonnet sequence was written in Spenserian stanza form, which Edmund Spenser created for his epic poem *The Faerie Queene*. Imagining the preborn baby as a tiny fairy guides the reader away from the medical term 'fetus' to the story of a developing child enveloped in mystical, magical wonder. Some of the most remarkable and latest discoveries we have made in the field of fetal development are integrated into the poem set, using reason and imagination to bridge the gap between medical knowledge and truth.

Each baby is created with a purpose. That purpose may be a mystery and a difficult calling to bear for the parents, but there is still a reason for that tiny life. I wrote these sonnets to inspire people to see the miracle of each child, unique from conception and created for a purpose.

Created

All is Darkness, but creation will come.
Infinite cosmos eternally planned.
Now void of substance, an infinite womb.
Then the Word brings light and life to the land.

A finite womb is purposed from the start,
To hold a life to touch the world anew.
With two, then one, to make new life apart.
A tiny hope, with destiny in view.

The universe from beginning shall be
Home to each spark of life in time's expanse.
Reach for the magic, seize the stars' glory.
The tiniest as priceless as the vast.

Imagined before time, conceived He knew.
Before the infinite dark, there was you.

Resources

To Connect with An Unexpected Journal

An Unexpected Journal is published quarterly; however, the conversation does not end. Join us on social media for discussion with the authors weekly:

***An Unexpected Journal* online:**
http://anunexpectedjournal.com

On Facebook:
https://www.facebook.com/anunexpectedjournal/

On Twitter: https://twitter.com/anujournal

On Instagram:
https://www.instagram.com/anujournal/

On Pinterest:
https://www.pinterest.com/anunexpectedjournal/

Comments and feedback can be submitted at
http://anunexpectedjournal.com/contact/
Be sure to sign up for our newsletter for announcements on new editions and events near you: http://anunexpectedjournal.com/newsletter

TO READ MORE

When discussing theology, or philosophy, or literature, or art, one is stepping into and taking part of a larger conversation that has been taking place for centuries. Each essay within the journal contains not only the thoughts of the individual author, but draws upon works and thinkers of the past. It is our hope that the writing not only engages your interest in the specific essay topic, but that you join us in the Great Conversation.

To read more, please visit http://anunexpectedjournal.com/resources/ for a list of the works cited within the essays of the journal.

SUBSCRIBE

Yearly subscriptions to *An Unexpected Journal* are available through our web site. Please visit http://anunexpectedjournal.com/subscribe for more information. For bulk pricing, events, or speaking requests, please send an email to anunexpectedjournal@gmail.com.

ABOUT AN UNEXPECTED JOURNAL

The Inspiration

J.R.R. Tolkien and C.S. Lewis, both members of The Inklings writers group, are well-known for their fiction embedded with Christian themes. These fantasy writers, who were also philosophers and teachers, understood the important role imagination plays in both exercising and expanding the faculties of the mind as well as the development of faith.

Beyond the parables of Jesus, their works are the gold standard for imaginative apologetics. The title, *An Unexpected Journal*, is a nod to the work to which Tolkien devoted much of his life, *The Lord of the Rings*.

Our Story

An Unexpected Journal is the endeavor of a merry band of Houston Baptist University Master of Arts in Apologetics students and alumni. What began as simply a Facebook post on November 1, 2017 wishing that there was an outlet for imaginative apologetics quickly organized by the end of the year into a very real and very exciting quarterly publication.

Our Mission

An Unexpected Journal seeks to demonstrate the truth of Christianity through both reason and the imagination to engage the culture from a Christian worldview.

OUR CONTRIBUTORS

Donald W. Catchings, Jr.
www.donaldwcatchingsjr.com

Donald W. Catchings, Jr. is Founder and Board Chair of Street Light Inc. and Pastor of The True Light Church in Conroe, Texas since 2009. Donald regularly contributes to *An Unexpected Journal* and has published various titles including his most recent release, *Strength in Weakness* — a Young Adult reimagining of the Theseus Myth.

Annie Crawford
www.anniecrawford.net

Annie Crawford lives in Austin, Texas with her husband and three teenage daughters. She currently homeschools, teaches humanities courses, and serves on the Faith & Culture team at Christ Church Anglican while working to complete a Masters of Apologetics at Houston Baptist University.

L.B. Loftin

Landon Loftin is a hospital chaplain and a Ph.D student at Faulkner University.

Christy Luis

https://www.youtube.com/c/ChristyLuisDostoevskyinSpace

Christy Luis has worked as a library assistant and currently runs a YouTube channel called "Dostoevsky in Space," where she talks about books and organizes public reading events. She has an Associate of Arts in Humanities and graduated cum laude from Regent University with a Bachelor of Arts in English from Regent University.

Julie Miller

Julie lives in College Station, Texas with her husband of 35 years and their dog Keeper. They have two married sons and two grandchildren. She recently earned a PhD in Humanities with an emphasis in Philosophy from Faulkner University's Great Books Program. She has served as a chapter director with Ratio Christi, a campus apologetics ministry, for almost 10 years. She is interested in issues concerning the philosophies of mind and human persons.

Annie Nardone

www.AnnieNardone.com

Annie Nardone is a two-year C.S. Lewis Institute Fellow with a Master of Arts degree in Cultural Apologetics from Houston Baptist University. She has homeschooled her three kids for twenty-five years and taught art and humanities at her local co-op. Her heart is for Rohan, Narnia, and Hogwarts, far fairer lands than this. Annie contributes and edits for *An Unexpected Journal* at www.anunexpectedjournal.com. She publishes online at www.literarylife.org, www.theperennialgen.com, and most recently began writing for the online magazine *Cultivating* at www.thecultivatingproject.com. She also wrote an historical cookbook for Bright Ideas Press. She can be contacted at: the.annie.nardone@gmail.com.

Megan Joy Rials

Megan Joy Rials holds her Juris Doctor and Graduate Diploma in Comparative Law from the Louisiana State University Paul M. Hebert Law Center and works as a research attorney in Baton Rouge, Louisiana. She is currently working toward an online Graduate Certificate in Literary and Imaginative Apologetics from Houston Baptist University. Her work has previously been published in the Louisiana Law Review, where she served as Production Editor for Volume 77, and An Unexpected Journal. She attends Jefferson Baptist Church with her family, and her main apologetics interests lie in storytelling of all mediums, fantasy literature, and the work of the Inklings, particularly C.S. Lewis and Dorothy Sayers.

Zak Schmoll

www.zacharydschmoll.com

Zachary D. Schmoll earned his Ph.D. in Humanities at Faulkner University and his M.A. in Apologetics from Houston Baptist University. He serves as the Managing Editor of *An Unexpected Journal*, a quarterly publication of cultural and imaginative apologetics. His academic work has been published in *Christianity & Literature*, *Mythlore*, *Cistercian Studies Quarterly*, the *Journal of Faith and the Academy*, and *Fourth World Journal*. His essays have also been featured at Public Discourse, Front Porch Republic, and The Federalist.

Jason Smith

www.woottonmajorpublishing.com

Jason Smith serves on the board of *An Unexpected Journal* and as senior editor for acquisitions and development at Wootton Major Publishing. In his spare time, he works a day job as a technical writer and marketing strategist for a medical device engineering firm, where he writes about fun things like FDA regulations and embedded cybersecurity. He is the pseudonymous author of the much-loved young adult fantasy series Fayborn and reviews every book he reads at *www.goodreads.com/mrwootton.*

John L. Weitzel
https://natureoftheself.weebly.com

John L. Weitzel has a Bachelor's in Psychology and a Master's in Counseling from CSU Long Beach, and a Master's in Theology from Loyola Marymount University. As of December 2020, he was advanced to candidacy for a Doctorate in Humanities, Faulkner University. John's Master's thesis at LMU was Christology of 1st Thessalonians. The working title of his dissertation is Augustinian Teleological and Freudian Nonteleological Mysticism in Times of Vicissitudes: Augustine's Interpretation of Imago Dei in City of God. He has taught at Marymount California University, Cypress College, and El Camino College. His most recent publication is Cosmology and Natural Law in Disney's Hercules. The research area of most interest to him is centered on pre-modern philosophy, especially Augustine, and the philosophy of personhood and psychology. He resides in Harbor City, California with his wife and three adult sons where they enjoy reading Tolkien and watching the movie adaptations directed by Peter Jackson. Story-telling and fairy tales are part of the family culture.

Thoughts from a Fellow Traveler

By Jack Tollers

If you aren't a Christian and have somehow gotten to the point where you are reading this, then I must warn you about the pebble in your shoe. For that is what it is like to be around Christians who discuss things together, whether or not they are "Christian kinds of things" that are discussed. At a certain point you will notice something about their point of view, something in their underlying assumptions, and to be honest when you do it will become quite annoying.

That is the pebble I was referring to.

But it gets worse.

Maybe it is not your fault that you happen to be reading this, and you've done a pretty good job milling about life without bumping into too much of this sort of Christian stuff. It could be the case that you haven't really made a conscious effort to avoid

Christianity, but chances are (if you are reading this) that is going to change. Somewhere along the line, perhaps even in the course of reading this journal, even, a pebble has worked its way into your shoe, and eventually the pebble will have to be dealt with.

It's not my job to tell you what it is. (I don't really know what "it" is in your case. All I know is that when the pebble got into my shoe, it got to the point where I couldn't walk much further without annoying my heel something terrible.) What I can do is suggest to you something that would have helped me if I had come across it in the back of some obscure journal: The pebble does not exist for itself. The pebble makes you stop and deal with the pebble. Stopping to deal with the pebble leads to thinking about your shoe. Then you start thinking about how much further up the trail you'd be if it weren't for that blasted pebble, which leads to thoughts about the trail itself and the path you're walking . . . and so on.

A particular Christian, or a particular thought expressed by a Christian, or perhaps just the particular quality you meet in places and things of Christian origin will eventually function to put you in mind of something beyond or behind themselves.

I say something because I'm trying to be non-partisan, but really I mean someone. Because at some point, the context for these thoughts will change to an awareness that this Christ person has been behind all of it.

When this moment comes, avoid mistaking Jesus for the pebble in your shoe. (If you do, it won't be long before another pebble gets in there and starts the whole thing off again. It took me years to figure that out.) Instead, consider the possibility that he is more like the path than the pebble. He said as much himself when he told Thomas, "I am the way, the truth and the life. No man comes to the Father except by me."

The truth aspect of Jesus' claim is, of course, exclusive. But there is more to his self disclosure. The other terms, "the way" and "the life" point us beyond a mere static assertion of fact or a single point of view toward a dynamic process of relational involvement. The pursuit of truth leads to knowing Jesus (if he indeed is truth incarnate). Thus, just as travelers come to know a country by living in it and exploring it, so people will grow in their knowledge of Truth as they make their way through life, the path itself bringing us in proximity to Jesus.

Such a journey, so conceived, is bound to take a person through some interesting experiences, and to unexpected places. Once the pebble is out of the shoe.

> All the way to heaven is heaven for he said, "I am the way" — St. Catherine of Sienna

> "And ye shall seek me, and find me, when ye shall search for me with all your heart." — Jeremiah 29:13

An Unexpected Journal

The Abolition of Man

Spring 2018   Volume 1, Issue 1

Subscribe to our newsletter at

www.anunexpectedjournal.com/subscribe

and receive a **free digital edition** of our first issue!

AUJ Issues

If you enjoy discussing faith, apologetics, and culture, don't miss an issue of *An Unexpected Journal*. Find this issues at your online bookstores, digital book sellers, or request your library to carry the journal.

For bulk, corporate, or ministry orders, please contact the journal at anunexpectedjournal@gmail.com

Yearly subscriptions and sets may be purchased at http://anunexpectedjournal.com/subscribe/

Volume 1 (2018)

Spring: The Abolition of Man

Summer: The Power of Story

Fall: Courage, Strength & Hope

Advent: Planet Narnia

Volume 2 (2019)

  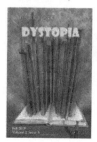 

Spring:	**Summer:**	**Fall:**	**Advent:**
Imagination	Film & Music	Dystopia	G.K. Chesterton

Volume 3 (2020)

Spring:	**Summer:**	**Fall:**	**Advent:**
The Worlds of Tolkien	Science Fiction	Medieval Minds	George MacDonald

Made in the USA
Middletown, DE
21 March 2021

35146503R00149